MIRACLES IN OUR MIDST

D0483782

TRUE STORIES OF DIVINE INTERVENTION

Contributed by Members
of Pine Lake Covenant Church

Edited by Susan R. Schlepp

First published by Dog Ear Publishing
4010 W. 86th Street, Ste H
Indianapolis, IN 46268
www.dogearpublishing.net

dog ear
PUBLISHING

ISBN: 978-159858-292-5

This book is printed on acid-free paper.

Printed in the United States of America

DEDICATION

To our Heavenly Father
and all who seek him

"Ask and it will be given to you;
seek and you will find;
knock and the door will be opened to you."

Matthew 7:7

PINE LAKE
Covenant Church

We exist to invite people into a relationship with Jesus Christ
that develops into a life of devotion to God and ministry to others.
We are a community of believers who are being…

Called

❖

Changed

❖

Gifted

❖

Equipped

❖

Sent

Real people being transformed by a real God.

Pine Lake Covenant Church
1715 228th Ave. SE.
Sammamish, WA 98075
Telephone: (425) 392-8636 Fax: (425) 391-2703
Email: office@plcc.org Website: www.plcc.org

TABLE OF CONTENTS

FORWARD

by
Pastor Tamara Buchan

God has many reasons for creating miracles. Many of those reasons are much bigger than our personal lives; God uses the miracles to do something much bigger than we can often observe. We rarely see the ripple effect of how the miracle will affect the lives far beyond those that we haven't even met.

However, God is clear that our response has to be one of praise. We must give God glory for the miracles in our lives. We do this by telling the stories to others. Sometimes it is humbling to tell these stories, but we must not stay quiet. When we do, God is not given the praise that he deserves.

When Jesus took his triumphal ride into Jerusalem and the people were praising him, the Pharisees told Jesus to tell the crowd to be quiet. Jesus' response was *"...if they keep quiet, the stones will cry out."* (Luke 19:40)

We must not keep quiet about who God is and what he is doing in our midst.

This book has been written so that the people of Pine Lake Covenant Church can fully give praise to God. We tell our stories so that the miracles are brought to the light to give God all the glory he is due.

Surrounded by Miracles

by
Susan R. Schlepp

How do *you* define a miracle? Ask ten people that question and you are likely to come away with ten different answers. Some see miracles all around us, in every breath that we take. Others see a miracle in the birth of a baby or in the complexity of how our bodies and the natural world function. Some define a miracle by degrees of magnitude, as being small, or large, or somewhere in between. Others reserve the term exclusively for the most unexplainable, jaw-dropping happenings. Sadly, some don't believe that miracles occur at all.

Webster's Dictionary defines a miracle as a marvelous event manifesting a supernatural act of God, or any amazing or wonderful occurrence. By definition, what constitutes a miracle is open to interpretation and debate.

Regardless of how we define a miracle, one thing is clear: Ask someone who has experienced one or more in their lifetime, and you will find someone who is never quite the same as a result.

This book is full of those *someone's* stories, ordinary people you might know from Pine Lake Covenant Church in Sammamish, Washington—courageous believers who were willing to come forward and share their life-changing spiritual events so that others may be uplifted and in the process, draw nearer to God.

Each of us is on a uniquely personal spiritual journey, believer and non-believer alike. It is thrilling to know that our dynamic, loving Lord is at work in the life of each and every one of us. Why, when, and how God chooses to intervene dramatically in an individual's spiritual journey is a mystery. Yet, it is undeniable that throughout history we have been and continue to be surrounded by God's miracles. We need only look to the many examples in The Holy Bible as proof.

It has truly been a blessing in my life to hear the stories contained in this book firsthand, to compile and edit them and to make them available for all to read.

From the outset, this book was a divinely directed project. When I completed the manuscript for my book, *The Reluctant Witness*, a divinely directed account of my spiritual journey to becoming a willing witness to Jesus Christ, I felt strongly that God was further instructing me to take some key chapters from my book, along with stories from church members, and compile them into this book. Still, I wanted to be sure.

Thankfully, early in the planning process, God gave confirmation of his direction when Pastor Tamara Buchan met with me at my home to discuss the vision for this book and the nuts and bolts of bringing it into fruition. I will never forget what happened at the end of that meeting.

While we sat at my dining room table, Pastor Tamara began to pray, and I bowed my head, closing my eyes. At once, I became aware of the supernatural presence of the Holy Spirit moving all around us. This was a sensation that I had experienced only once or twice before in my life when I had been in the presence of Pastor Tamara when she prayed.

What made this time particularly incredible was that when she began to thank God for my calling to work on this project, suddenly a tremendously heavy, invisible force descended through the ceiling, dropping down on top of me. The incredible weight of it seemed to force my body down lower into the chair. Surprisingly it was not an uncomfortable feeling, but definitely an overwhelming and inescapably spiritual one.

As the weighty force pressed down and enveloped me, I told Pastor Tamara what I was experiencing. She asked if it was an uncomfortable feeling. After I assured her that it wasn't, we continued to pray. Afterwards, the mighty weight was slowly and completely lifted from me leaving me speechless wondering what had just happened.

Pastor Tamara explained that she believed that I had likely experienced Shekinah, the Hebrew term for *the glory of God*. The word *glory* in Hebrew: *kabhod* literally translates to *heavy*. She felt certain that God had just anointed me for this project. Not only was I filled with a renewed desire to publish this book to the glory of God, but I also had a greater sense of the power and majesty of our creator. The incredible experience pushed my understanding of God to a completely new dimension—literally. I had to chuckle to myself; thank goodness God doesn't choose to reveal himself to us in this way all the time, or we wouldn't be able to function at all!

I am so grateful and thankful to Pastor Tamara Buchan for her unwavering support, wisdom, guidance and prayers, which were instrumental in this project becoming a reality. I would like to thank the body of Pine Lake Covenant Church for embracing this project, and for the prayer warriors who diligently and faithfully prayed through the tremendous spiritual battle that was won by the power of the Almighty God released through prayer. Thank you to all of the contributing writers and to everyone who assisted with the administrative aspects of the book.

It is my sincere hope that the stories courageously shared by the members of the body of Pine Lake Covenant Church in *Miracles In Our Midst—True Stories of Divine Intervention* will draw you into a deeper relationship with God. I pray that the stories will truly be a blessing in your life, as they have been in mine.

Faithfully in Jesus Christ,

Susan R. Schlepp

DIVINE ENCOUNTERS WITH ANGELS

Praise the Lord, you angels, you mighty ones who do his bidding, who obey his word.

Psalm 103:20

Along for the Ride

by
Pastor Reid Olson

In the summer of 1991, while driving on Interstate 5 from Walnut Creek to Bakersfield, California, I had my first encounter with an angel. I was a youth pastor in Northern California and had just driven the camper truck home after Family Camp wrapped up in beautiful Lake Tahoe and was extremely exhausted. My friend, Todd, called me that day from Bakersfield to tell me he had his first opportunity to preach in his church that next morning on Sunday. He asked me to come down the next day to listen and support him.

I knew that the drive down would take about five hours and being as tired as I was, I wasn't quite sure I could make it; but I wanted to try. I knew Todd would do the same for me. So as soon as I parked the trailer at the church, ran home to grab a change of clothes and some fast food, I was off. I left the hardtop of my 1966 MGB convertible in the garage at home thinking the wind would keep me awake, and besides, it was a crystal clear evening with a clear forecast for the weekend.

About two hours into the trip, the sun had set, and I found myself drifting in thought to the beautiful stars above. A thought went through my mind that if God made this stellar setting for the evening drive, as I gazed at the stars, then he must be as real as what I was seeing. I began to speak with God about whether he existed or not. I was foolishly bold enough to ask him to prove himself somehow.

"Lord, if you're really out there, then would you show me something like a shooting star?"

No sooner had I finished my thought with the Lord, than an amazing array of brightness rocketed across the horizon, and I found myself bursting into tears. I felt shame for asking the Lord for a sign at the same time as feeling a sense of awe for the God who would honor my request.

I think the awe of God responding to my prayer overpowered my sense of shame soon enough because with another sense of foolish boldness, I asked God, "Are angels real? Would you show me an angel?" While I somehow remained on the road at seventy miles per hour, driving through tears, the Lord answered me again. I looked at the passenger seat where an illumined figure was now along for the ride.

I don't know how I remained on the road, as I gazed at this passenger for longer than I can remember. He was wearing a shining white garment and appeared to be over six feet tall, with dark hair. His feet appeared to be going through my overnight bag on the passenger seat floorboard.

I was overwhelmed now with a sense of peace, as I gazed at this angel in my car. He didn't say anything; he just smiled with a peaceful look on his face. I continued to drive along Interstate 5 south toward Bakersfield and found my composure had become calm and composed again. I don't remember taking my eyes off him. My boldness before the Lord reached a new high, or a new low, depending on your view, as a thought came to my mind to ask the angel himself about the Lord. As soon as I took my attention off the Lord and asked this angel what it must be like to dwell in the realm of heaven with God, he vanished.

I had much to think about for the duration of my drive. I spoke with the Lord, as I continued on my way to Todd's home, and God comforted me along the way. I made it to Bakersfield safely late into the night, more than fully awake at how the Lord and I had interacted along the starry night somewhere along the Interstate 5 South.

A Child of God
to Call Our Own

by
Lauri Kraus

When I think of our family's journey to have a baby, the only word that comes to mind is purely and simply a *miracle*. My husband and I waited for over nine years for an answer to our prayers for a child to bless our life together. Finally, we decided that our desire to be parents was so great that adoption was the road we should take. We consulted an adoption attorney who told us to meet with a social worker to become approved as potential parents. Then we could search for birth parents that were ready to place their child for adoption. We were anxious to take the next step in finding a child who would be our own.

One night I had a vivid dream that an angel came to me. A woman with long, straight, dark hair and rosy cheeks wearing a white dress was sitting on the edge of our bed. She looked at me and said, "I am an angel sent from God to tell you that your baby is going to be born very soon. All he asks of you in return is that you raise him in the Christian faith." Then she was gone.

I woke up knowing in my heart that at anytime we would be parents. Everything was going so well with our adoption process. We placed an ad in the newspaper, and before we knew it, a potential birth mother contacted us. She said she would be giving birth in six weeks and was in the process of choosing the right parents for her unborn child. We told her all about us and our desire to adopt a child into our family. She said she wanted to talk with other families and assured us that she would let us know very soon what her final decision was. We hoped and prayed that we would be the chosen ones.

Two weeks later, she called to say that she had chosen us. We were thrilled by the news. She asked if we would like to pick up our daughter at the hospital when she was born. My husband and I gleefully accepted. We could not believe how quickly our prayers for adoption had been answered. Those two weeks were filled with anticipation and preparation for the arrival of our new child into our home.

Finally, the long two weeks were behind us. The day had finally arrived to pick up our baby daughter. We were nearly bursting with joy, but our bubble of happiness was about to explode in disappointment and heartbreak. We were in for a tremendous surprise and letdown. Instead of a new baby, we discovered that the woman we had put our trust and faith in was not a potential birth mother at all. Instead, she was a forty year old, lonely soul who had never been pregnant. Apparently, she was desperate to find someone, anyone, who would befriend and comfort her in her depressed and lonely existence. During our correspondence with her, she never asked for money. Later we found out that we were not the only victims of her sad scheme for attention.

My husband and I felt limp and used from this experience, but I continued to recall the amazing dream of the angel's visit. I kept the faith that God would come through with the promised child. Despite the emotional roller coaster the woman had put us through, I felt only pity and empathy for her. I believe that God had a hand in this too.

It was only one week later that we received a call from another birth mother who said she was seven months pregnant and needed a family for her child. Following so quickly on the heels of our sour experience, I was hesitant to believe that this could possibly be real. Once again, I remembered the divine dream and promise. Did I dare hope again?

On January 13, 2001, we went to meet the potential birth parents at a fast food restaurant in Monroe, Washington on an evening when it was actually *not* raining. I was so nervous and excited at the prospect of adopting a real, live, baby this time that I completely forgot to ask what the birth mother looked like on the phone, so that we could easily find her when we met. As I entered the restaurant, I began looking around at each customer. Everyone was seated, so I couldn't tell who was pregnant. Remarkably, the first table that I approached turned out to be the birth parents. I was relieved to see that this time the birth mother really was pregnant!

We talked for a long time that evening and were elated when they asked us what we planned to name our new son. We had already decided on the name Zachary, if it was a boy, meaning *remembered by God*. The birth parents asked us if we would use the name, Paul, as a middle name, after a beloved cousin of theirs. They went on to say it was the name they would have chosen, had they decided to parent the baby themselves. My husband and I quickly agreed. We thought it would be very special for Zachary to have part of his birth parents with him always. As a lucky coincidence, Paul, was my father's name.

This time the adoption process couldn't have gone smoother. The birth parents allowed us to be present for the prenatal visits and for the birth of our son on March 9, 2001. Today we remain in contact with them and are so very thankful that they gave us this priceless gift.

When we brought Zachary home for the first time, that night I rocked him gently in my arms. In this perfect moment, I thought back to the angel who had visited my dreams to deliver a divine message of hope. Suddenly it occurred to me that the day she came to my bedside was the exact day that our son was conceived—purely and simply, a miracle.

A Divine Appointment

by
Gayle Larson

Sometimes the Lord sends us an angel in human form to come to our aid when we need it most. I experienced this after I had been a Christian for a couple of years, when I was living on Lake Washington in Renton with a girlfriend. When I awoke that morning, I found that it had snowed the night before and the roads were sure to be a challenge for my little, blue Pinto. I headed off to work at 7:00 a.m. At the time, I was an administrative assistant for an architectural firm in Seattle. When I got to the overpass for the freeway, I pulled over onto the shoulder because it was too slippery to continue safely. I decided to walk back to my apartment and wait for the temperature to rise and the roads to clear up.

I called my employer and told them I would be in later that morning then spent some time reading the Bible and praying. For some reason, I decided that I should go back out to my car at 10:00 a.m. At the appointed time, I walked back to my car, got in, and turned the engine on.

All of a sudden, seemingly out of nowhere, a car pulled onto the shoulder directly behind mine. Right away, a man came to my driver's side window. What struck me about him was his size. He was huge, almost like a giant! The next thing that struck me is that he was serious and didn't say a word when I rolled down my window. I told him that I needed a little push to get onto the freeway. Looking back it reminds me of a verse from the Old Testament book of Judges 13:6 *"...A man of God came to me. He looked like an angel of God, very awesome. I didn't ask him where he came from, and he didn't tell me his name."* Immediately he left without saying anything, got into his car, pushed my car onto the freeway and was gone in a flash. It was almost as if he disappeared into the chilly air.

As I drove on to work, it seemed to me that this enormous, solemn man had been sent to that on ramp at the appointed time of 10:00 a.m. specifically to come to my aid that morning. I will never know whether this man was actually an angel, but I do know for sure that no concern is too small for God. *"For he will command his angels concerning you to guard you in all your ways."* Psalm 91:11

Why I Believe In Heaven

by
Laura J. Nelson

Growing up, my family rarely attended church, but somehow I believed in God. I mostly prayed to him in emergencies. I wanted to believe in heaven, but I wasn't sure that there was life after death. If there truly was a heaven, I reasoned, then good-hearted people must end up there. I focused on having a positive attitude, being kind to others and having fun in life.

In 1992, my uncertain faith in God and heaven changed dramatically, when I witnessed three miraculous events in the midst of the most heartbreaking experience I have ever endured. It all started on July 1, 1992. My husband, Brian and I were in a delivery room at a hospital in Bellevue, Washington waiting for my obstetrician to induce labor on my very pregnant body. To pass the time, we shared with each other how happy and excited we were to meet our new baby. We wondered what he or she would look like and be like. While we were waiting, a nurse hooked me up to a machine to monitor our baby's vital signs. Immediately she knew that something was terribly wrong. Our baby's heart rate was critically slow. She rushed to find my doctor and within minutes, our second child, Wendy, came into the world by emergency cesarean section.

Sadly, Wendy was not breathing at birth. Artificial respiration brought her back to life, and she was moved to the neonatal intensive care unit of the hospital. Wendy was weak and could not perform any major functions on her own, such as sucking and swallowing. A narrow feeding tube was placed down her nose and into her stomach to feed her. The doctors delivered the tragic news to Brian and I. Wendy had severe neurological damage and would not live long.

Despite the medical complications, Wendy was a beautiful little baby. I instantly fell in love with her. I couldn't believe we had a daughter this time, but she was not supposed to turn out this way. She was supposed to be strong and healthy. I was heartbroken and in shock. I wished with all my might that somehow I would wake up, open my eyes and find that this nightmare was just that—a nightmare. I would find Wendy completely healthy. But this was not to be. Instead, I opened my eyes to find our critically sick baby beside me and felt my heart fill to overflowing with sadness and deeply felt love for her.

At two weeks old, Wendy was transferred to a hospital in Seattle. After several tests, the doctors concluded that the umbilical cord had been pinched on and off during the last week of pregnancy. The resulting lack of oxygen caused such extensive damage that Wendy would eventually die of pneumonia. It was only a matter of time.

Wendy needed constant care and would not be able to go home with us. Completely devastated by the news, Brian and I visited her every day. Friends and relatives also visited to offer support. Together we held her, hugged her, sang to her, bathed her and clothed her. Each day I put a tiny bow in her hair. It became our mother-daughter ritual, however short it would last. As Wendy clung to life, we gave her all the love we could give knowing each moment with her was truly a gift. After six precious weeks, Wendy died. Even so, I felt like I had loved her for a lifetime.

Throughout this heartbreaking experience, three miraculous events happened to profoundly change me. Many people, including the prayer chains at two of my in-laws churches were praying for us. Although I didn't have much faith or knowledge in God, a mysterious phenomenon happened to me beginning when Wendy was about one week old. Suddenly I could feel God encircling me completely with love, peace and comfort. Without a shadow of a doubt, I knew that God was right there with me, and I believe that he must have come because of all the prayers that others had prayed on our behalf. It was strange that at the same time my heart was grieving over the condition and impending loss of our daughter, I was also being comforted and surrounded by so much love. As a result, I became a believer in God's magnificent presence and the tremendous power of prayer.

During this time, a devout Christian woman came to visit Wendy and me in the hospital with a girlfriend of mine. She assured me that our baby would go to heaven when she died and would be healthy and happy up there. She said that Wendy would be playing in a green grassy field surrounded by beautiful flowers and trees. Jesus would be nearby watching over her. Unlike her short, earthly life, the sun would always be shining for Wendy in the afterlife with God. This was the first time I envisioned what heaven might be like.

My sister-in-law also visited the hospital. She is a Christian who also had no doubts about the existence of heaven. She reassured me that there is a wonderful eternal life for those who believe in Jesus Christ as their Lord and Savior. She talked with me on the phone and assured me that the Lord God loved our family and would never leave us. She believes in John 3:16 from the New Testament which states, *"For God so loved the world that he gave his one and only Son, that whoever believes in him shall not perish but have eternal life."* She told me to put my trust in Jesus Christ and say, "Forgive me." It was at this very moment that I asked Jesus into my heart and turned my life over to his loving care.

Later I read an eye-opening book called, *Within Heaven's Gates*, by Rebecca Springer. It was about her extraordinary visit to heaven. I also read, *The Light Beyond* by Raymond A. Moody, which was about the near death experiences of millions of people. After experiencing God's presence each day and learning about countless others who have seen a glimpse of heaven, it opened up my thinking even more. I realized there really was a possibility of eternal life. Several people I asked said they truly believed in heaven and their faith fascinated me. I wanted to have the same deep trust in a glorious after life as they did.

My Christian friends and relatives believe that the Bible is the true Word of God. Their viewpoint on heaven is explained in 2 Corinthians 5:1–7 which states, *"Now we know that if the earthly tent we live in is destroyed, we have a building from God, an eternal house in heaven, not built by human hands...Now it is God who has made us for this very purpose and has given us the Spirit as a deposit, guaranteeing what is to come. Therefore we are always confident and know that as long as we are at home in the body we are away from the Lord. We live by faith, not by sight."* I took comfort in this.

The second astounding event that occurred during those painful weeks was when Wendy was almost six weeks old and clinging to life by the thinnest of threads. While walking into her room one day, I observed four small angels hovering above her. The angels were talking among themselves, and I could see right through them. Even though I couldn't make out what they were saying, I intuitively knew they were discussing Wendy.

Brian and I had been spending the night in Wendy's hospital room because we knew she was going to die very soon. She had been medicated for two days so that she would not feel any pain. The medication caused her to be limp and very sleepy. She had only opened her eyes halfway a few times in the previous forty-eight hours. At 5:30 in the morning, I picked her up and laid her down on my chest. Our tummies were touching each other and her arms were dangling down at my sides. If felt so nice to cuddle with her. I cherished every moment, as I listened to her breathing. About an hour later, a third miraculous event occurred. As her limp body lay against mine, suddenly Wendy turned her head, gave me a little kiss and a very strong hug and then she was gone.

I will never forget that one, perfect hug. It was so miraculous and mysterious. There was no possible way that she could have hugged me in her condition, even if she had been wide-awake and not on any medication. I truly believe that this goodbye hug was a gift from God to help me say goodbye to our sweet daughter and know that she would be taken care of eternally.

The miraculous goodbye hug, reading about countless people who have experienced a glimpse of heaven, and knowing that eternal life is clearly indicated in the Holy Bible, has given me the true faith I had been searching for. I have also found it in the mysterious presence of angels above Wendy's crib for two days, and being surrounded by God's immense love and peace for five weeks. These events confirmed to me that there truly is a wonderful life after death to look forward to for those who believe in Jesus Christ. My life would never be the same.

Since becoming a Christian, I no longer have the deep sense of loneliness in my heart that I did for so many years. My heart is filled with love, peace and caring about others and myself. I have more joy, more purpose and more meaning in my life than ever before. If I hadn't lived through it, I never would have thought that in the process of losing our precious daughter Wendy, I would gain eternity.

Food for Thought

by
Maxine Miles

When our children were younger, we always spent Labor Day weekend boating and waterskiing in Eastern Washington. On this particular day, we were returning with our ski boat hitched to the back of our aging station wagon, when the radiator started to overheat. Our car was literally lurching west along Interstate 90. Not knowing if we were going to make it home, we pulled into a rest area to let the car cool down and try to add water to the radiator.

While my husband and I attended to the car, our daughter and her girlfriend who had accompanied us that weekend went up to the rest area building. Within minutes, they ran back to tell us that there was a lady with a baby up there that needed food and money because their car had broken down. Not knowing quite what to think, but not wanting to put a damper on our daughter's enthusiasm for helping others, I searched through our leftover dry food items, dug through the cooler, and came up with some things I thought could be used: such as milk, bread, cold cereal, and margarine. The thought did cross my mind that we might need the food for ourselves if our car broke down later on the highway, as we still had a substantial drive ahead of us. But I brushed it aside having faith that we would eventually make it home.

After gathering the items, I walked up with the girls, and we gave the bag of food to the woman who was young, quite slim, and had medium length hair. From what I recall, the baby wasn't old enough to walk yet and was resting in a baby carrier. I told the woman that although some of the things had been opened already, all of it was still good. I explained that we too were having car problems and didn't know if we would even make it home that night. Then she said something that seemed strange to me at the time, "You don't have to worry. You will make it home without any more problems." I thought it was extremely odd that she would make that statement with such confidence and authority in her voice. It was as if somehow she knew for certain what our fate would be that day.

Still a little puzzled by her statement, I went back to the car, while the girls stayed behind. A few moments later, they came running down and said that the lady with the child had disappeared. The girls had searched the parking lot from one end to the other and couldn't find them anywhere. Then we all loaded back into the car and began the remainder of our drive. Much to our surprise and relief, our car ran smoothly all of the way home. Although it was still very hot outside, our old station wagon showed no signs of overheating again. Oddly, it was as if nothing had been wrong with our vehicle in the first place.

As I have thought about this occurrence over the years, I have always questioned whether the woman in need was a person, or an angel put there by God to see what his people would do to help a stranger. Would they give willingly from the heart or would they turn away? I'm reminded of the Bible passage from Hebrews 13:1–2 "*Keep on loving each other as brothers. Do not forget to entertain strangers, for by so doing some people have entertained angels without knowing it.*" I'm awfully glad that we did something to help but have wondered if we should have done even more.

He Commanded His Angels

by
Marie Gidcumb

"If you make the Most High your dwelling—even the Lord, who is my refuge—then no harm will befall you, no disaster will come near your tent. For he will command his angels concerning you to guard you in all your ways; they will lift you up in their hands, so that you will not strike your foot against a stone." Psalm 91:9–12

An eerie silence gripped the city of Bethlehem, making it seem like an old abandoned town that was long forgotten. Bethlehem was under complete military lock-down by the Israeli Defense Force (IDF) with a full twenty-four-seven curfew imposed on the ancient city. No one was allowed to leave their homes except during a three to five hour break one day each week to purchase a few groceries, check on other family members, and briefly tend to any medical, dental, or pharmaceutical needs. The quiet was often disrupted by military tanks rumbling through the city streets, gunfire, explosions from grenades or bombs, and low flying helicopters patrolling the area for would be antagonists.

Several months had passed since Charles and I answered God's call to serve as missionaries in war-torn Bethlehem, arriving during the height of the Palestinian uprising in 2001. Just one year prior, on a vision trip there, we visited a peaceful Bethlehem. Tour buses and tourists lined the bustling streets, cars scurried by with cheerful drivers honking and waving at friends and tourists, and children laughed and played on the sidewalks. Now the city lay in ruin. A terrible silence slithered through each broken pathway like a shadowy force, penetrating the walls of every home and infecting the inhabitants with foreboding, depression, and hopelessness. Heavy drapes were kept tightly drawn in every window, and doors remained locked in every business establishment and family dwelling. Snipers took aim and fired at anyone who dared to look out any window or door.

The ancient city was tightly sealed. Blocks of concrete as tall as a single story dwelling closed the entrance to Bethlehem at Rachel's Tomb. Mounds of debris barricaded all other roads leading in or out of Bethlehem. Remnants of shelled buildings, and walkways crumbling from the weight of military tanks, gave testimony to the physical battle raging in that historic little town where Jesus was born. With the ongoing cycle of violent exchanges between the Israeli army and the Palestinian militant groups, the Holy Land became unholy.

Peering out a protected window of our flat at the Bible College where we taught, I watched a plume of smoke from a recently shelled building rise into the air, and my thoughts took me back to the first whisper of God's call to the mission field. I was somewhat reluctant then, reminding my Heavenly Father of my physical limitations. Having asthma was my primary concern. My physicians repeatedly warned me not to test the things that triggered an allergic reaction. I tested anyway, and I always failed. With this in mind, I hounded the gates of heaven, praying, "Lord, what if I fail again? What if this isn't in your will?" Ah! Such a little me!

God's answer to each petition, however, was always the same: "Trust Me." I finally chose to trust. Joy and peace flooded my heart the instant I said, "Yes." Traveling to the Holy Land, in complete surrender to his will, my soul fastened tightly to the Shepherd's leading. While serving in Bethlehem, I experienced God's mighty hedge of protection from all the allergens and irritants that triggered many violent asthma attacks in previous years. God provided his protection in many other wondrous ways. In this story, I will share two other experiences.

Bethlehem's early evenings are especially quiet as the bulk of the IDF withdraw for the night and jeeps with armed soldiers patrol the empty streets. On a few rare occasions, the soldiers lift the curfew in the evenings so families can visit each other and shop.

On one particular curfew-lifted summer evening, Charles and I decided to stroll around the corner and a couple of blocks away to check on a sick friend. It was a superbly beautiful and peaceful evening with the sunset glow illuminating the rooftops and silhouetting the buildings against a golden sky. After days of stale indoor air, the soothing gust of a gentle breeze refreshed us. Delicate wind-whispers and bird songs drifted softly in the air, wrapping around us like a joyful embrace.

Suddenly, and without warning, gunfire cut across our path in both directions, in front of us and behind us. We were half a block away from the Bible College where we lived and served. The college, sandwiched between two refugee camps, is frequently patrolled by the IDF. It is usually safe to venture out during a curfew lift. However, most of the conflict between the Israeli soldiers and Palestinian militants takes place in these camps. One never knows when a hostile encounter will take place.

As the gunfire continued, we became disorientated by the shock of this sudden, violent action and didn't know which way to turn. All at once, and from out of nowhere, a small army of children surrounded us. They encircled us three to four children deep, and they appeared to be from five to eight years of age. They spoke excitedly as they pressed in around us, moving us in the direction they wanted us to go. "Do we go this way?" I asked. They nodded approvingly and smiled as they parted the way for us to walk through. We took a couple of steps and then turned to thank the children, but they were nowhere in sight. They left, as quickly as they came. In that extraordinary moment, these words from Psalm 91:10–11 came to my thoughts, "*then no harm will befall you, no disaster will come near your tent. For he will command his angels concerning you to guard you in all your ways…*"

Curfew was less enforced on the city after a time. The citizens were given a promise, by the Israeli government, assuring them that the imposed closure of the gates to Bethlehem would open for Christmas. Two Christmas seasons without the customary celebrations in ancient Bethlehem, weighed heavy in every heart and dampened every spirit. The promise of a long-awaited Christmas celebration renewed everyone's hope. Rejoicing and preparations for the forthcoming celebration took place throughout the city. A news correspondent for a major TV network interviewed us for a Christmas special that aired on Christmas Day 2002. Celebrating the Christmas interview with us, missionary friends joined us at a local restaurant where we enjoyed a wonderful Mediterranean dinner and great companionship.

A multitude of stars graced the evening sky when we said goodnight to our friends. Whenever nighttime settled on the city, we had to be especially careful, stepping over broken concrete, rocks, shattered glass, and other debris. It was a very chilly evening. I decided to walk on, a little ahead of Charles, with my hands tucked in my pockets to keep them warm. We were a few yards away from our flat when the toe of my shoe caught in a wide crack in the sidewalk. I stumbled. To my dismay, my left foot was hung up in the pant cuff behind my right foot. With both hands stuck in my pockets, it was impossible to maintain my balance. Charles was a few steps behind me, too far away to help. I was falling face first into a large pile of jagged rocks. "This is really going to hurt!" I thought.

In the next moment, however, I remembered that the Lord's plans are to prosper me, not to harm me. Jeremiah 29:11 *"For I know the plans I have for you," declares the Lord, "plans to prosper you and not to harm you, plans to give you hope and a future."* My face was inches away from the rocks. Suddenly I was gently lifted up by unseen hands and then softly placed down again on both feet. The incident was such a surprise that it nearly took my breath away. God's angels were at work again. Psalm 91:12 *"...they will lift you up in their hands, so that you will not strike your foot against a stone."* I turned around to see Charles with a look of amazement on his face. "Did you see that?" I asked. He nodded affirmatively. We both witnessed God's promise in action. Before continuing our journey home, we joined our hands in prayerful thanksgiving.

Months earlier, when we were getting ready to leave for the overseas mission field, several people commented on how brave we were to serve in a war-torn country. My response was always the same, "We're not brave. We're obedient." A fearful spirit might have kept us home; and it might have prevented us from starting a ministry of prayer and encouragement with oppressed and despairing Christians in the Holy Land. However, we chose to trust the Most High and to make him our dwelling and our refuge, and he honored our obedience.

Heaven Sent

by
Margaret S. (Peggy) Hendricks

I think it was a *core* of angels, who had been assigned to watch over me that summer day in August 2000. I had been at a medical clinic for a physical therapy session and was driving myself home along a curving two-way street at the southwest side of Lake Sammamish. Suddenly I was sharply jolted, as my car came to a grinding halt against a low stone retaining wall on the opposite side of the street. I immediately recognized that I had experienced a total blackout. My car had crossed the lane for oncoming traffic and had ended up nearly on top of the retaining wall, which separated the street level from a steep drop off down to the lake's edge. From where I sat, it was not a pretty view!

I turned the motor off and tried to open the door beside the wall. Before I could get out of the car, there were two people at the door beside me. They had been following behind me observing my weaving driving and knew I was an accident about to happen. When they determined that I had no visible injuries, I told them about the heart failure episode I had been hospitalized for only a few weeks before. The man and wife turned out to be off-duty medics on their way home from work and happened to have a canister of oxygen in their car, which they immediately applied for my breathing. They also took my blood pressure and called 911, knowing I would need to go back to the hospital that I had just come from.

When the paramedics got there, the same couple that had stayed with me helped me from my car into the ambulance. Realizing I was at risk for heart failure, the paramedics immediately transferred me to their oxygen supply, and we headed back to the hospital. By the time we arrived, I was going into congestive heart failure.

I have never had trouble believing in God's providential care for his own. This incident was total proof to me that the two people, who were right behind me with oxygen in their car, were truly God's angels sent to watch over me that day.

I found out later that the blackout had been caused from medication I was taking. While my car was totally gutted underneath from hitting the retaining wall, the accident could have been much worse had there been traffic coming around the curve in the opposite direction—another blessing that day. Fortunately, our insurance provided the replacement car that I am still driving today.

While I didn't learn the names of the couple that had come to my aid, I hope they know that they were God's special angels watching over me that afternoon.

Summoned by Name

by
Gayle Larson

As a young child, I attended church and was baptized. I went through confirmation in about sixth grade and confessed a belief in God. However, I did not know about asking the Lord into my life as my personal Savior. At one point in my childhood, I remember reading the Bible with my Dad. I specifically remember Psalm 91:1 *"He who dwells in the shelter of the Most High will rest in the shadow of the Almighty."* Years later as my mother and I stood in a hospital recovery room watching my Dad as he came out of open heart by-pass surgery, he started quoting that same verse. I was flooded with the memory of my Dad and reading that verse together many years before.

Reflecting back, I can see how God's hand and influence were at work in the significant relationships in my life, especially my grandmother, who nurtured the seeds of faith that were planted in me as a young child. Sometime in my teen years, my family quit attending church. As a young adult, I went the ways of the world.

Later, I had an experience that has taken years to fully realize the significance of. When I was twenty-one years old, I was hospitalized because of a mental breakdown. Reacting to my sense of hopelessness, I remember the doctor telling me to have faith. My Dad had been praying for me and had other people of faith praying for me during this time. As I awoke one morning, I was coming out of a dream that I had died. I heard the beautiful voices of multitudes of angels calling me by my name. It was the most indescribable, incredible, melody of voices that I had ever heard. For a long time I kept this in my heart and did not tell anyone what had happened.

I recovered from the breakdown and continued to go on with my worldly life. God placed people in my pathway to pray for me and influence me during those years. It wasn't until four years later at the age of twenty-five that I grew tired of my lifestyle. I met a young spirit-filled woman who worked in the same building as me. I was attracted to her because of her joyful countenance. She invited me to a large Christian conference in Seattle. While I was there, I noticed a group of young Christians who were full of the joy of the Lord. I knew they had something that I did not have, and I wanted it too.

At the end of the week while sitting in my car outside of the townhouse I lived in, my friend helped me to pray a prayer to ask the Lord into my life. At the end of the street was a dead end sign. That night, I dreamed that my life had been on a dead end street, but now I had come to a new life in Jesus Christ. This is what the multitude of angels was calling me to four years earlier, when I was in the depths of despair. It took years pursuing my own desires, before I was ready to repent and release my life to the Lord.

What a change I experienced as I became a new person in Christ! I knew that the angels were now greatly rejoicing that I had finally turned back to God. I had accepted Jesus Christ into my life, and my life would never be the same! *"In the same way, I tell you, there is rejoicing in the presence of the angels of God over one sinner who repents."* Luke15:10

Now that many years have passed, I am able to reflect back on this miraculous intervention with more insight as to the full meaning for my life. I am reminded of the Bible verse from Isaiah 43:1 *"But now, this is what the Lord says—he who created you, O Jacob, he who formed you, O Israel: Fear not, for I have redeemed you; I have summoned you by name; you are mine."* This scripture cements in me the powerful truth that God desires every sinner to come to repentance and salvation. Thankfully, God is patient with us in our process to accept his gift. *"The Lord is not slow in keeping his promise, as some understand slowness. He is patient with you, not wanting anyone to perish, but everyone to come to repentance."* 2 Peter 3:9

A Heavenly Push

by
Doug Barlow

It was December 1991. I worked in an office building nine miles from my home. There were forecasts of a big snowstorm heading our way. My plan was to beat it home by leaving work as soon as I finished my last meeting. As I came out of the conference room, I saw through the windows that I was too late. A combination of snow and freezing rain was already coming down hard and piling up on the roads. Driving was going to be difficult. I called my wife, Holly, to tell her I was coming, but just got the answering machine.

I rushed to my old minivan as best I could; I was on crutches, having shattered my toes in an accident the week before. My tires were a bit past their prime, but I did have front wheel drive. I joined the creeping traffic, hoping my commute, typically twelve to fifteen minutes, wouldn't take more than an hour.

My home was on a plateau on the other side of a lake from my office. To get there, I had to go around one end of the lake or the other, and then take one of only several possible routes up onto the plateau. My favorite route used smaller roads and a steep hill. I decided that wasn't my best bet, given the conditions. I headed for the longer route with larger roads and a less steep hill.

Traffic was painfully slow, barely moving at a creep. While waiting, I prayed that Holly and my two kids would get home safely and that God would give me the ability to drive safely in this mess. After over an hour, I reached the base of the hill, and found out why traffic was so slow—the school busses had tried to go up the hill to get the children. One after another, they had spun out, and now a handful of them were completely blocking the road.

Traffic was slow because we each had to pull forward far enough to see that further progress was impossible, turn around, and begin our creep back toward other routes. We could also see that power was out on the plateau; the freezing rain had pulled down the power lines.

After two hours on the road, I stopped at a fast food restaurant for a break. The manager had turned it into a travelers' aid station, giving out hot coffee and letting people use his phone. I tried calling home again, but once more got the answering machine. This worried me; it was starting to get dark. If the school busses hadn't been able to pick up my kids, would they walk home? That was possible, since it wasn't that far. I could imagine them ignoring the phone. But where was Holly?

My kids had just received some Christmas candles as a gift. They were only eight and ten years old and not that fond of the dark. If Holly wasn't home and the power was out, would they try to light their new candles? We didn't yet trust them with matches. I was very worried and started out again. By this time, the glut of traffic had been joined by the normal rush hour crowd, making travel almost impossible. I headed for my favorite route, hoping it was passable. For the entire two and a half hours it took me to go five and a half miles, I desperately prayed for protection for my wife and kids and to keep them safe from fire and cold.

As I reached my favorite road up onto the plateau, I could see there was no hope there. Cars and trucks had taken turns trying to make it up the steep hill, only to spin out and slide to the side. The hole between stuck cars had gotten smaller and smaller, until it was plugged. The design of the immobile cars on the hill reminded me of a Christmas tree.

I considered abandoning my vehicle; at that point, home was barely a mile away. But I couldn't see any place to park my minivan with the sides of the roads already clogged with abandoned cars. Picturing trying to go a mile up a frozen hill while on crutches further dissuaded me. I continued on to the next road up, still desperately praying for my family's safety and for God to give me the driving skills to get home.

Suddenly I heard a voice: "I'm sending angels to push." So much for God's opinion of my driving skills! This wasn't the first time I had heard God speak, so I recognized the voice. However, it happens rarely enough that it is still unsettling. I had plenty of time to think it over, as I crept towards the next road up the hill.

When I got there, I was pleased to find it was not yet completely blocked. I watched as one at a time, cars would attempt the hill. A few made it, but most just slid to a stop as their tires spun wildly, then came back down and moved on. I waited my turn. The line of cars waiting to try their luck made it impossible to get a run at the hill, and there were plenty of vehicles in the ditches lining the road. So there wasn't much room to maneuver.

My turn finally came. I started out like everyone else and came to the spot a third of the way up the hill, where most people lost traction. I could hear my wheels spinning. My speedometer and tachometer jumped way up. My wheels were just spinning freely with nothing to grip. I kept moving, steady and in a straight line. Miraculously, I was being pushed! I checked my mirrors to look for the angels, but there was nothing to be seen. I cruised past four-wheel drive vehicles abandoned in the ditch, and crested the hill, shouting praises to God.

Once on top, I had hoped traffic would be lighter, but apparently, there were also other ways up the hill. I joined the next queue, my car bouncing with me as I burned off the excitement and excess adrenalin. About one and a half hours later, I came to the next hill right in front of my church. Again, I waited my turn to attempt the hill. This time I didn't see anyone making it. Again, with wheels spinning, gauges flailing and me shouting "Thank you, God!" over and over, my car went smoothly up and over the crest of the hill.

I had been closely surrounded by heavy traffic for the last seven hours. The sides of the roads had been clogged with abandoned cars. All the headlights around me had made it easy to see my surroundings. As I went over the top of the hill, everything changed. All the power was out, and everything was dark and silent. I could see the snow-covered road only as a gap between the dark trees. There were a few abandoned vehicles here and there and a solitary truck at the bottom of the hill, vainly struggling to go up. Once I passed him, I felt completely alone; nothing looked familiar.

I continued on, trying to figure out exactly where I was. The ground was relatively flat from here to the last big hill on which we lived. I was getting close to home, and my excitement was building. I continued praying for my family. Suddenly the trees fell away on my right. I realized it must be the grocery store near my house where I needed to turn.

It was difficult finding the roads in the dark; but there was no one else to be seen, so I could take my time. I crept along looking for cross streets in my headlights, until I found my final turn. I headed up the last hill, again steady and straight. I began to worry about my driveway because it sloped down to the garage. I wondered if I would I be able to stop at the bottom without crashing through the garage door.

The headlights illuminated a very familiar tree on my left. I realized I was in front of my house and the driveway was just ahead. I thought to myself, "I could make it from here even without angels!" Instantly the car slipped, spun, and came to a stop, stuck in the snow. I found myself parked on my lawn. Next to me was a freshly shoveled driveway, with an open garage door at the bottom. I should have let the angels finish the job!

I got my crutches and hobbled into the house, where my whole family warmly greeted me. They hadn't answered the phone because they were outside keeping the driveway clear for me. We compared timelines. When God told me he was sending angels matched up with when my family took a break to stop and pray that I'd make it home safely.

DIVINE INTERVENTION

So do not fear, for I am with you; do not be dismayed,
for I am your God. I will strengthen you and help you;
I will uphold you with my righteous right hand.

Isaiah 41:10

Miracle in Kodera

by
Larry Larsen

I'm sure for a lot of you, like me, it is much easier to look back on something and say, "Now I can see God's hand in that event." Sometimes it might be twenty years later, or if you are also like me, I am convinced that it might be when we get to heaven and have a "seminar" with God. He will allow us to see his plan unfold in a situation here on earth that we had no clue of why it was happening at the time.

Let me tell you of an incident in Kodera that I believe God let us see some of his insights into in a relatively short period. As you know, Pine Lake Covenant Church (PLCC) has an ongoing partnership with a community in Kenya on the Western side of the country called Kodera. This community has a population of about four thousand, but isn't even on a Kenyan map. It's located west of Lake Victoria and a just north of the Serengeti Plain. We are involved in this community primarily because of Christopher Sure, a local Kenyan who came over here to study at Trinity Bible College, just down the road from us. We have been involved for over five years now, primarily with improving their school, building a playground at the school, providing medical teams, building a health clinic, holding spiritual conferences, and improving their water supply and sanitation. Before we were involved, other humanitarian efforts were attempted, but nothing ever got accomplished because of corruption and bleeding off of the money into the pockets of dishonest and evil men.

Now enters Christopher and a committee of Christian men and women in Kodera in partnership with PLCC. You can imagine that the noses of the evil men were out of joint when the money was now actually going into projects that accomplished something positive and not into their own pockets. Threats were made on Christopher's life and all sorts of obstacles were thrown in the way of this community moving forward. The evil culminated a year and a half ago when a team of twenty-four of us went over. The first week was primarily a Medical Clinic week and then the medical team came home. Twelve of us stayed on to do spiritual conferences, painting, and some additional medical work. Since this community is below the equator, our day would start when it got light about 6 a.m. and end when it got dark about 6 p.m. After dinner, we would sit around Christopher's living room in a circle for our daily devotions and review the day's activities, before heading off to our tents for a night's rest.

On this particular night, as we were sitting around the living room, I saw a sawed off shotgun entering the door followed by a semi-automatic rifle. Then a voice said, "Everybody get down on the floor!" At first, I thought this was a joke, but then I thought, Christopher wouldn't joke like this. Suddenly a group of men burst into the room and began ransacking the house, stealing watches, cameras—anything of value they could find. Amazingly, they didn't find our passports, money or airline tickets. My wife, Priscilla, had been praying that they wouldn't find them, even though they were in plain sight. I was on the floor with a gun to my head, while the men searched each of us and took what they could.

While the twelve of us were lying on the floor, we began praying out loud. My prayer was, "Lord, get these guys out of here!" All the while, the evil men were yelling, "Be quiet and stop praying!" Our prayers clearly bothered them. But their threats didn't stop us. We kept right on praying out loud. I was proud of our group. In the worst circumstances, not one person panicked or lost faith.

Then they took Amy Glover from our group outside at gunpoint. After about a minute passed, I heard a gunshot and feared for the worst. The gunshot woke up the community and the evil men decided to make a run for it by stealing Christopher's car. I thought they were going to shoot us all because when they initially came in, they weren't wearing masks and we could identify them.

John who lives next door to Christopher heard the gunshot, ran over and found us all on the floor. He said, "Get up and run because they are coming back!" Hearing this, we scattered in all directions. Erika grabbed my hand and said, "Larry, please don't leave me." I grabbed her and Brandon and we ran across some nearby fields and hid. All at once, we started hearing a high piercing noise, and I thought our attackers had gone crazy. What it turned out to be was the women of the community sounding the alarm with their tongues and yelling, "They're killing the Mizungas!" which means *white people*. Later we would call them "our angels of protection."

Things began to calm down, and we felt that one of us should sneak back and see what was going on. Brandon did this and came back and told Erika and me that it was OK to return. As we walked back across the fields to Christopher's house, I could see in the darkness what looked like about two hundred people. Hearing the alarm, concerned members of the community came out of their homes and gathered around armed with spears, clubs and machetes. When we approached, the group opened up, like God parting the Red Sea, so we could walk into Christopher's house closing up after we were safely inside. They formed a protective circle around the house.

I saw Priscilla sitting on the couch and you can imagine the rush of emotion that I felt at seeing her safe. I rushed to her and gave her an enormous hug. Then to my relief, I saw Amy sitting on the bed in a back room. I walked back, gave her a hug too, and said, "Am I glad to see you!" Christopher's nineteen-year-old niece who he and his wife Florence are raising was sitting next to her. It was then that Amy told me that his niece had been raped. Making a horrendous event even worse, the man who had raped her said he was infected with the AIDS virus.

Amy went on to tell us of her own harrowing ordeal. How she had been forced out of the house at gunpoint by some of the evil men. After some discussion, one of the attackers let it be known that he was going to rape her. Amy thought, "I am ready to die, but I'm not going to die this way." It was in that moment that she decided to run. Into the darkness she ran, recalling where one of the gates in the yard was located. One of the attackers fired a gunshot toward Amy that thankfully missed its mark. Amy fled to the neighbor's house, finding safety inside.

After the attackers fled, we tried to contact the police. They arrived in about an hour. With my adrenaline pumping, I was ready for our US Embassy to send in a helicopter and fly us out of there immediately. At about 1:00 a.m. the District Commissioner and his armed guards arrived. They provided security for us that night, but informed that they couldn't provide it for the rest of our stay and we should leave first thing in the morning. None of us slept much that night, although later Priscilla said I snored. At daybreak, we started breaking camp. The local people that had provided the initial protection were there watching us pack up and I'm sure wondering if they would ever see us again. Priscilla gathered them all around us and told them the story of Joseph being sold into slavery in Egypt and how what evil men had meant for harm, God turned it around and made good come out of it. She assured them that we would be back, that somehow, some way; God would bring good out of the night's tragic events.

We left and were provided by God with a place of refuge and recovery. Since the attack, PLCC did indeed return to Kodera. I am happy to report that since returning, the community is stronger than ever. The local committee is functioning stronger than before. A new church has formed that is a true joy to behold. The medical clinic is progressing faster than we had anticipated. A large tent that we provided is being set up to temporarily seat two hundred and fifty worshippers, until the church building can be completed. Land has been purchased that will be the site of the new church and a new private school that is going to be called, *Pine Lake Academy*. Classes have begun in a temporary building, and over one hundred children are already attending. An ultra sound machine and light microscope are now in place at the medical clinic, which has greatly improved the health of the community. Since the arrival of the equipment, there have been no infant or mother deaths during labor and delivery. In addition, two local nurses are on sight at the clinic full time to provide care for the community.

In the time that has past since the attack, we were especially relived to learn that Christopher's niece did not get pregnant from the rape and does not have the AIDS virus to date. She has been receiving trauma counseling and is doing very well. She is currently studying to be a pharmacist.

I could go on about the miracle that is happening in Kodera since the attack that night, but suffice it to say that the work we are doing at PLCC for Kodera is making a difference and we have been privileged to be on the front lines of God's battle.

The Miracle of Life

by
Helen Boyer

My first born, my daughter Lisa, was almost three when I started trying to get pregnant again. Our attempts for two years were not successful, and we eventually started treatment with an infertility specialist. We went through nearly five years of various high-tech medical interventions and periods when I took hormones of different kinds. It was an emotional roller coaster every month, and our efforts continued to disappoint. Finally, I had had enough. The hormones warped my system, and I felt out of alignment. The diagnosis was of early menopause, and the medical outlook was not optimistic.

I gave up. I mean I truly released my desire to have another child. I decided I had been blessed with one beautiful child, and I was happy with that. I did not need more. With a sense of great relief, I went off the hormones. By then, my daughter Lisa was a member of the church choir. We were attending Emmanuel Episcopal Church, which began each service with a ceremonial procession into the sanctuary. The acolytes would lead, followed by the priest. Then the choir, fully robed in blue and singing, would follow. The beauty of this pageant always moved me to tears.

In fact, at that time, I could not stop crying during the entire service. Each Sunday, I would cry fairly steadily for an hour and a half. I usually sat near the front, and the kindly pastor would sometimes watch me weeping through his sermon. We never spoke about it, so I have no idea what he made of my persistent tearfulness. I didn't know what to make of it myself. I wasn't aware of feeling any particular sadness; I just had to cry. The beauty of the presence of God in that place was just overwhelming.

This went on for some months. Then one day about six weeks after I had stopped the infertility treatments, I became pregnant. My doctor could not believe it. "How did this happen?" she asked. "You tell me," I answered.

That child, my second born, was my son Nicholas, whose name means: "Victory to the people." This is how I told him the story of his birth when he was young:

> *Before you were born, my eyes were dry for a long time.*
> *Then I went to a church where people walked with God in*
> *rows, wearing long blue robes and singing songs of*
> *praise. My eyes cried and cried, and all of the sadness*
> *drained out of me. And then you came into my body to fill*
> *me up with gladness. You were a blessing from God. Your*
> *sister Lisa was one of the singers that had made my heart*
> *cry out the sadness so that there would be room inside me*
> *for you to grow.*

The Nativity has always been very moving to me. I still can't hear the song *Silent Night* without tearing up. I love birth and new life. In retrospect, I understand that God was readying me during those seven years to understand that it is God who grants us life and blesses us with children. First, I had to release my desire and my attempts to manage the process and let God control. When I was prepared, God performed a miracle and gave me a child.

A Walk Toward Hope

by
Anonymous

During the end of my eighth grade year and through the summer, I gradually became depressed. A friend of mine, who has since become my best friend, recognized it before I did. She noticed that I was always down and was not enjoying what I usually loved to do. Most of the time, I wanted to cry. I began talking to my friend over the phone almost every night, but just felt worse and worse.

I had been riding and learning to train a horse for my trainer and stable owner. In the fall of my ninth grade year, he brought home a new "project horse" for me. At first, I thought this horse was crazy. She was high strung, not well trained, and hadn't been ridden in years, except for an occasional trail ride. I wanted to train her and ride her. My trainer gradually taught me to work with her. He encouraged me to experiment, to discover for myself what worked with her and what didn't. It was at that time that God created an awesome connection between the horse and me. Training her gave me purpose.

Even so, in the fall of that same year, I was still getting deeper and deeper into depression. I began to cut myself, for when I could inflict physical pain on myself, the pain inside of me went away. I was also becoming suicidal. My best friend told someone for me and my parents found out, and then began the hundreds of doctor appointments and counselor visits. What no one seemed to understand was that it wasn't just clinical depression I faced, but spiritual warfare harder than I had ever known.

By January, I was very close to committing suicide; the only thing that stopped me was God. On January 20, the day before my birthday, my parents came and picked me up from school in the middle of the day without warning. They had decided to drag me to the ER. Apparently, it was the fastest way to get to a psychiatrist. I don't think I've ever been that angry with my parents in my entire life. While waiting forever in a tiny room with a small bed and a chair and no windows, I answered the shameful questions repeatedly. I text messaged my best friend to tell her why I wasn't at school anymore. I scared her to death. After the psychiatrist visit, I got fast-food dinner, and then my parents dropped me off at youth group.

My sister had told a friend, whom I've known my whole life and is like an older sister to me, that I was depressed. She came over and asked me how my day was going, so I told her. She had to go pick up another girl who lived a couple minutes from the church, so I went with her. Since we were a little early, we cried and talked in the car. It was at this time that God told her to take me to a certain place. Now it's kind of funny because this *certain place* was where she had first learned how to pull over on the side of the road when she was learning to drive. So that is exactly what she did—pull over.

It was cold and it started to snow, and God gave her words to say to me. She pointed backwards and said, "Depression is back there." Then she pointed forward saying, "Hope is that way." When she said this, she pointed directly at the light post that was a ways down the deserted street. Then she said, "Do you want to go there?" and of course I said, "Yes!" without knowing what I was getting myself into. Then we got out of the car, linked arms and began to walk step by step through the slush and snow. She told me, "Each step you take is a step closer to hope." I kept walking. When we finally reached the light post, I had hope like I had never had before. "You did it!" she said, and I smiled through a veil of tears. She hugged me and since we were now late for youth group, we left to pick up the other girl and drove back to church.

After we arrived at church and dropped the other girl off, we decided that after such a huge spiritual event we should go to the back of the room and talk about the experience rather than go to youth group. When youth group was over, we told one of the pastors and my parents what had happened. Afterwards there was a lot of crying, and then we went home.

I've had hope ever since that day, and that hope has saved my life. I ended up buying the horse I was training. I love to work with her and barrel race her. All things weren't immediately perfect, and never will be. My best friend can testify to that. But with my hope in Jesus Christ alone, I can keep fighting all the spiritual battles I must face throughout the rest of my life, for I am not alone, and Christ will win in the end.

This verse is one of my favorites from the Bible. Isaiah 40:28–31 *"Do you not know? Have you not heard? The Lord is the everlasting God, the Creator of the ends of the earth. He will not grow tired or weary, and his understanding no one can fathom. He gives strength to the weary and increases the power of the weak. Even youths grow tired and weary, and young men stumble and fall; but those who hope in the Lord will renew their strength. They will soar on wings like eagles; they will run and not grow weary, they will walk and not be faint."*

Walking to the light post, toward hope that day, I soared on the wings of an eagle. I know all my life can't be spent on a mountain-top, for the valleys make the mountains what they are. After all, what is soaring without first walking and running? I put my hope in the one who will see me through even the worst of storms, and you can too.

A Practice of Faith

by
Dr. Ralph Aye

When I started practice in surgery years ago, most doctors worked for themselves and started their medical practice by taking out a loan to pay overhead and all personal expenses until the practice grew. That's how I started. Although my wife Kathy and I had never tithed ten percent to the church, we began to do so at the beginning of my practice, tithing on all income, though we were getting deeper and deeper into the hole.

Several years later, as the practice grew, we, and our accountant, sort of lost track of the income, and wound up owing over twenty thousand dollars in taxes-money we didn't have. Suddenly and unexplainably there was a big blip in my practice, and we had just enough, almost to the penny, to pay the tax. Then the practice settled back to where it had been.

A number of years later, we had a serious medical issue with our daughter, which was not covered by insurance, and the monthly expenses were far more than we could afford. While fluctuations in medical practices are common, as in most businesses, my practice suddenly exploded, to the point that it was hard to keep up with the work, and this continued for the entire eight months that she needed care. Again, we had enough to cover the expenses. Then things slowed down again.

Of course a skeptic might explain away these unusual upturns in business as sheer coincidence; but the magnitude of them, the timing, and the sense of peace that Kathy and I both experienced, made it clear to us that this was God's provision. Over the years, we have not always been the best stewards of our resources, and we've never had much extra, but we've continued to tithe, and God has continued to be faithful in providing for us, on many other occasions not quite as dramatic as these.

Networking with God

by
Ed Morin

In the late 1980's, while working at the University of Washington, I discovered the profound power of the Internet. This was before it had become a household word, and I knew that for my tiny online Internet mail and news service, Northwest Nexus, to succeed, we needed a direct Internet connection like the University of Washington had. We did eventually get one (another miracle story in itself), but it was really expensive, in part because of the costly network equipment that was provided as part of a turnkey service provided by one of the few companies managing the Internet commercial backbone at the time. As time went on, I realized that for my company to grow, we needed to get our own core network equipment and be able to eventually support more than one "backbone" connection to the Internet.

Unfortunately, for us to do that would require some very expensive Internet backbone equipment of our own. Specialized network routers such as these normally cost about forty thousand dollars *each*. At that time, that sort of money was equivalent to several months of gross revenue and my wife, Charlotte, and I just didn't have that kind of money lying around to speculatively invest in the business.

Charlotte said "Well, the Bible says that God owns the cattle on a thousand hills (Psalm 50:10), so I'm sure he can provide one of these routers for us."

I responded a little flippantly, "Well, I don't think that many of these high-end routers have ever been made; but if you really believe that, then pray for *two*, so we'll have a backup in case the first one fails." Reliable networks should always have backup gear!

For the next year, we prayed, and I asked everybody I met if they knew of any "cheap Internet backbone routers" we could get. Most folks laughed me off saying "Yea, right!" or "In your dreams!" and similar retorts. That is, until one day when I visited a local, up-and-coming cellular phone company. I was helping them with their Internet connection, and I jokingly asked my standard, "Know of any cheap Internet backbone routers I can have?" question. Lo and behold, the guy replied seriously, "Well, yes, I think so!"

I was blown away and asked him to show me what he had. It turned out that he had a pair (*yes, two*) of the exact routers we needed; they were just sitting on the floor in his office! They had been sitting there for about a year because they were part of a complicated insurance settlement that they had been working out.

As the story went, about a year prior, a rack of equipment had been routinely shipped to a location in Southern California for installation, as part of their network expansion. It was a standard rack of equipment, which included the network routing gear I was after, as well as many other pieces all pre-installed and configured for the remote location. Many of these standard network equipment racks had been sent to various network locations, as they worked to expand their cellular data network. As with all the other racks, this one was routinely packed and sealed in a huge wooden crate, insured and sent on its way, as had been the case with all their previous shipments.

It made it to the destination in its wooden crate, unloaded from the truck and received. From the insurance photos I was shown, the crate looked undamaged on the outside, which was why it was routinely received. However, when they later went to uncrate the equipment to install it, to their horror, they discovered that the entire rack of equipment—some two hundred thousand dollars worth of gear including the network backbone routers—was terribly mangled. The gear had been severely damaged *inside* the crate, even though no external damage had been apparent whatsoever! That was the basis of the insurance dispute, and it took a year for everybody to sort it out.

The insurance company finally agreed to pay to replace the routers, after they couldn't get the local router manufacturer office to agree to fix them. The "broken" ones were sitting in this guy's office and, as of a few days before I got there, had just become the property of the insurance company because of their settlement. The routers had a few large gashes on them, but otherwise looked intact inside. He also said that he had straightened out some bent metal on them, but he had not tested them. He gave me the insurance adjuster's contact information to "work out a deal" for the routers and anything else that was left that I might want. He wanted it all out of his office as soon as possible!

I contacted the insurance claims adjuster to find out what he expected to get for the damaged equipment. When the guy asked me what I was willing to pay for them, I wasn't sure what to answer. One of my business partners had advised me to remember that "you can always go up in price, but you can never go down." We beat around the bush a bit, and it eventually came out that they hoped to get five to ten cents on the dollar in salvage value. I could afford that! We ended up getting the entire pile of gear that was leftover from the insurance claim for less than five cents on the dollar, or about five thousand dollars in total, including the *two* Internet backbone routers we had been praying for!

But that was only part of the story; we still didn't know if they worked! First, I tried dealing with the local router manufacturer's office. They were well aware of the "damaged" gear and refused to help us claiming that the "backplane was warped" and that they were irreparable. We were brokenhearted to have come so far only to seemingly arrive at a dead end.

Just a few months before acquiring these routers, Charlotte and I had purchased a cargo pallet loaded with a few dozen leased-line modems from the surplus store of a large, local aerospace manufacturer. Given the nature of our business, I knew that we would eventually need them, so we bought the whole pile on the cheap with Charlotte's employee discount on top!

One Sunday afternoon after church, Charlotte and I decided to see if the routers worked. I had acquired a manual for the modems and figured out a way to make a simulated leased line. Using some old wire and resistors and two modems in a back-to-back configuration, we hooked up the two routers to each other. This was another advantage of having two of them: they could be tested by talking to each other. We didn't even have any equipment manuals for them yet so we had to work blindly. To our amazement, they powered right up and started working!

Since the local router manufacturer's office wouldn't help us, I decided to call their headquarters in the Bay Area and talk with their national service department. I explained about the potential shipping damage and, much to my delight, they were happy to repair anything needed for a small fee. They also said that since the routers appeared to work as they were, we could simply put them on a maintenance plan for a nominal monthly fee—sight unseen. Now we could get maintenance *and* repair anytime we needed! It eventually turned out that one of the routers did have a circuit board with an intermittent problem, but it was quickly and easily replaced under our maintenance plan for no additional cost.

These two Internet backbone routers became the cornerstone of our entire regional network infrastructure that enabled us to eventually become one of the largest Internet service providers in the Pacific Northwest. We supported hundreds of businesses large and small, and thousands of individuals on a network stretching from Bellingham, Washington to Salem, Oregon, and as far east as Coeur d'Alene, Idaho and west to the Olympic Peninsula. At the end of 1998, we successfully sold the company after having achieved yet another year of record revenue and over four thousand percent growth over the previous five years which had landed us on the *Puget Sound Business Journal's* "Top-100 Fastest Growing Companies" for three consecutive years (1996, 1997 and 1998)—a feat few companies ever achieve.

Had it not been for the Lord's miraculous provision several years before, we never would have gotten our business off the ground let alone achieved the success that we did. God really does "own the cattle on a thousand hills." Except in our case, it was Internet routers instead of cattle!

Escape to a New Life

by
Anonymous

Anyone who has ever been in an abusive relationship, whether emotional, verbal, or physical, knows how debilitating it can be. It is my sincere hope and prayer that my harrowing experience will help and inspire others to take the first courageous step out of a bad situation.

I was married to my ex-husband for twenty-five years. During that time, I often dealt with harsh and degrading verbal assaults, which sometimes escalated into physical attacks. Despite the abuse, I took my marriage vows to heart and was determined to somehow work out our problems together. Desperate to turn the situation around, I begged him to join me in therapy. He flatly refused.

At the time, I didn't realize that I was married to a sociopath and narcissist—a man who was completely devoid of a conscious. Over time, I learned that many of my symptoms that I attributed to depression and the oppression of living day-to-day with such a person were exacerbated by the fact that he was secretly and viciously drugging me with Halcion, which is regularly prescribed for the short-term treatment of insomnia. The high doses that he frequently slipped into my juice caused extreme forgetfulness and often knocked me out for extended periods. Unknowingly I was living life in a virtual daze.

Over time, I became trapped in a vicious cycle. My ex-husband would use these drug-induced handicaps as fodder for further proof of my ineptness as a human being and spouse. Consequently, my self-esteem was almost non-existent. The abuse escalated, and soon it became apparent to friends that my health was in serious jeopardy. They urged me to leave him, but I was adamant that I would never get a divorce. I had to concede though that separation did seem like the only way that I could survive this dreadful situation.

When he found out that I had consulted an attorney to discuss my options, he became enraged. For the next two years, he did and said abhorrent things to me in hopes that I would be the one to file for divorce. He was determined that I should take the "fall" for the failure of our marriage. He saw nothing in his own behavior that was abusive or out of line. When I refused to give up on us, he resorted to giving me higher and higher doses of Halcion.

One night he slipped five or six times the prescribed dose into my juice. Yet, miraculously the drug had little effect on me. Amazingly, I could remember when I should have had no memory at all. I could breath, when I actually felt like I was about to take my very last breath. I awoke precisely at 6 a.m. the following morning fresh and alert, when I should have been nearly comatose. I attribute this to the intervention of a close friend whom God had awakened that very night to fervently pray for my well-being. That morning was a turning point for me. Now I could muster the strength to do what I thought I couldn't do—leave the marriage for good.

When I look back with more clarity, I see how the Lord brought me through all those devastatingly lonely years and through the subsequent years of re-establishing my life with my children, as a single parent. It was the hardest period of my life, when I quite literally didn't think that I could survive the betrayal and the injustices of the legal system. Little by little, day-by-day, with God's grace, my faith was restored.

Today I am joyfully celebrating a new marriage to one of my best friends and a true life-partner. I know to the depths of my soul that the Lord watched over my children and me during all of those dark years, when I was in the grips of a twisted man in an abusive marriage. I am so grateful that God miraculously intervened that night. As a result, I found stores of hidden courage to tap into and clear-headedness that allowed me to escape that old life and start anew. Truly, my life is a testimony to God's transforming power to turn what man intended for evil into blessings, which prove his great love for each one of us.

The Lord is Calling

by

Priscilla Larsen

Back in early 2001, most everyone was getting scam email from a supposed person in Africa whose estate was worth millions of dollars, but it was impossible to settle the estate unless they found someone to simply agree to have the funds transferred into their bank account in America, then provide access to that bank account, etc. Finally, that "Good Samaritan" would be rewarded with a large compensation. I would quickly dump the email and get on with my life.

One day, an email arrived to me through the PLCC office, from a "Brother Foley" in Accra, Ghana that simply infuriated me. All I could see was that someone had put together all the heart wrenching horrors that could be done to a person and then expected the recipient of the email to jump to their help and send money. How did I get that letter? Because someone kept calling the PLCC office collect over and over again, and no one in the office was willing to take the collect call from Ghana. Someone finally gave the operator the church email address and asked this person to send an email explaining what they wanted. They then sent on that email to me. This letter made me so angry; I just knew it was a scam with a capital S.

The email told of such horror—of the Charles Taylor Rebel Army finally arriving in Monrovia, Liberia, demanding that all people return to their familial home and wait. They began going house-to-house interrogating the families, and inflicting such horrors on them, as they deemed fit. They arrived to the home of a former policeman turned pastor and evangelist, his nurse wife, and their five children—Foley's home. They began searching for a supposed gun in the home. When they could not locate it, they began making horrendous demands on his father to perform in front of the family, such as I will not describe here. When he would not comply, they cut off his extremities and left him to die. They then went to rape the youngest daughter, and when the mother stepped in to defend her, she was beheaded, to which the oldest children ran to her defense and were shot. This now left the two youngest children, a boy and a girl, who were beaten and left for dead.

God sent a lady from next door to check on the family. When she found the two children, she took them home with her. Ultimately, they were forced into service to the Rebels, and for the next four months, they simply tried to survive until the ECGMOG, Africa's Peace Keeping Force, arrived in Monrovia to rout the Rebels. When told about their situation, a captain in the force took these two youth down to the cargo ship in harbor bound for Accra, Ghana and asked that they be taken there.

The next four days on board the ship were spent reading their father's journal to see if he might have noted down someone they could contact when they reached Accra to get help. In their search, they found written in that journal the name of PLCC, the office phone number and Pastor Chris Breuninger's name. In retrospect, I believe an angel could only have written it there because Pastor Chris never met a Liberian pastor in his life!

When they arrived in Accra, they were met by a Christian man, another angel, who took them to his poor home, gave them some food, and helped them learn how to make a collect phone call to America. Hence, the multitude of collect calls, none of which were being answered, and they were getting more and more desperate.

Finally, the church did what they should never do—give out a personal phone number of one of their members. Later I received one of these collect calls in my home. However, I was not there, so a young man who lived with us did what he should not have done—

take the collect call, and tell this person I was not at home. This prompted a very angry response to Foley's original email to the church ending up with my telling him that if he was in truth a refugee that he should contact World Vision in Accra, and I gave him the email address. I told him that he had contacted me completely across the world from where he was and there was no way I could help him from here. I added that if he was a believer in Christ, then I knew God would help him find help. I signed off with "God bless you." and thought, "That is the end of him!" Only to receive an almost immediate reply saying "What do you mean that God is bothered by distance in helping his little children? Put your spiritual mind to work and find a way to help us," which infuriated me even more—the audacity of this person preaching at me!

I was in the office when another collect call came in, and I was asked to take it. I was chairperson of our Global Missions Department at church, hence the "logical one" to take the call. I was still angry, and my first thought was to ask how old he was, expecting him to be an adult who should be able to care for his little sister. He told me that he was seventeen, and his little sister was only thirteen. Oh my, what a melting happened to my heart and mind! Suddenly, here was a real life need, and I didn't even have a clue on how to reach out and meet it. In that moment, my heart broke. I asked how I could help, knowing that he certainly didn't have a bank account. Where would I send money? His response was, "Western Union!"

Well, I probed a bit, and found out that this man, an angel who had met them at the ship had given them a bit of food, but he was too poor to be able to help them much. I told him I would send him fifty dollars US via Western Union, and he was to do three things:

1. Pay back the man who had helped him and then go buy some food.
2. Take a bus to Accra and find a Christian Church. I was sure they could find help there.
3. Find someone who could corroborate his story for me.

Then I dusted off my hands, confident that this was the last I would hear from them. I was sure that they had probably sent this same scam email to a lot of people, many had bought it as had I, and he had made lots of money. Now he was out of my life! But God intervened again and the first person they encountered was a woman. They told her they were looking for a "Bible believing Christian Church" and she, another angel no doubt, took them to her church and to her pastor.

Then 9/11 happened on Tuesday. By Sunday on my way out to church, the phone rang. I answered it, and became angry again. Foley was on another collect call, saying he had a man for me to speak with. I answered in a very angry voice, "Why should I believe you? You are probably part of the scam! Who are you anyway?" After a short silence, his answer rang true, "I am a Christian Pastor of a small Christian Church in the midst of a Muslim community and we are trying to reach the Muslims for Christ." Wow, that was no scam answer!

And so our relationship began. He promised to find a school for the kids, and get back to me. He kept his word, put them into a boarding school with the promise that I would pay for the year. Now all this time, my husband, Larry was very upset with me. What a waste of money! What a scam I had bought into! What a mess! I kept telling him it was not his money that I was spending; it was my mother's inheritance, and she would be happy with my choice. Then I kept right on answering emails from Ghana, when I would receive them.

Soon, the two were calling me "Mommy" and writing to tell me about school and what they were learning, and such gratitude they showed. I began to believe that they were for real and became determined that I would visit them in Ghana to see for myself. Larry's response to that request was, "Sure, you can go, but I'm not." However, his advice was for me to first contact our longtime missionary friend who was born and raised in Ethiopia and Ghana and had returned as a missionary for many years. I sent him the emails I had first received from Foley, and told him of my placing them in school and that now I wanted to go and see for myself if this was all legitimate.

He responded to me from Ethiopia that very day, encouraging me that many former missionaries return home having seen such tremendous needs and because they could not help them all, they would choose not to help any. His counsel was always, "If you can help just one, then help." He gave me the email address of the Sudan Interior Mission Guest House in Accra, Ghana and told me to tell them we were friends, and we could stay there.

Suddenly, Larry decides he too should go visit them! And that is what we did. We flew over there, met them, saw their school, their church, their city and fell in love with them. They were so hungry for parents that Cynthia took hold of Larry's hand and hardly would let go the whole time we were there. We learned more of their story, saw what God was doing in their lives, and were so terribly impressed over the beautiful spirit which God had worked into them in spite of all the tragedy they had experienced in their short lives. So, we have helped them complete four years of school, get passports again, get established in Ghana, and they are beginning to develop into delightful Christian adults who are seeking to serve the one who is the father of the orphan—God.

Let me bring you up to speed quickly now. In the past five years, Foley, a young man who has heard God's call on his life to become a pastor and evangelist like his father, has in fact founded a Liberian refugee church, at the Refugee Camp outside of Accra. There are about two hundred and fifty in attendance, and we have been blessed to help build this facility for them. There is another family in our church who has heard the call to help financially many times, and this has been such a help in their lives. God has impressed Foley with a dream, which he has dreamed three times now. In the dream he sees himself back in the backwoods of Liberia, standing on the front porch of an orphanage he has founded, looking across the street to the church that has sprung up under his care. He is convinced that God saved them because he has a long term plan for their lives.

I have truthfully never known someone who is more filled with gratitude to God for even the terrible things which God allowed in their lives. Foley is grateful also that God brought them a new set of parents. He is convinced that God's plan is good and God will work all things together for their good because they love the Lord and are called according to his purposes (Romans 8:28), even though God has allowed Cynthia to contract tuberculosis.

In fact, that is what we are dealing with right now. We have had to have Cynthia hospitalized for the past six weeks, and she has just returned home to the apartment we have helped them get. She will be on medication for the next six months and will need to build herself up again. Foley is committed to being her nurse and making certain she survives even this!

The long term plans include sending Foley to Bible School,

after he gets his sister cared for adequately. He would like to become a pastor, and if God leads them, return to Liberia to serve Christ as he will call them.

Freed from the Ties that Bind

by
Anonymous

It happened one January day in 2005 around noon, when I was preparing a special dinner for my daughter and my grandson, who both have January birthdays. We planned to celebrate that evening, and I had made several trips to my freezer in the garage. There is a side gate on my home that locks, but that day it was unlocked because I made a trip or two to the garbage can.

As I went in my back door, suddenly two women pushed their way in right behind me. One of them sprayed my eyes with pepper spray and dragged me into a chair in the living room. Later I learned that the police thought they had been hiding in the garage until I went inside my home.

I asked them numerous times what they wanted, and they never would answer. Several times, they came back and sprayed my eyes. It really burned them. Then the oldest one who was pregnant took a big silver wrench and hit me on the head several times. I was bleeding quite badly. They dragged me from chair to chair and got blood on most of my furniture. They didn't seem to care at all that I was bleeding. The police said they were both high on methamphetamine.

Finally, they got out some electrical cords that they had brought with them. They tied me up with two different cords. The younger girl was so strong. She came back and cinched the cords tighter. Then they threw me in the bathtub and left the room. While I was in the tub, they opened the bathroom door and sprayed me with a fire extinguisher, which smells awful. My grandson told me that it takes the oxygen out of the air, and my bathroom is small. I do believe they tried to kill me.

I said prayers while a lot of this was happening.

As I lay in the tub, suddenly I heard a divine voice in my ear telling me to lock the bathroom door. I was amazed to find that miraculously my bindings had all fallen off. Somehow, I was able to muster the strength to climb out of the tub and lock the door. Shaking from shock, I found a blanket to wrap up in and sat on the floor. Then I prayed a specific prayer that God would send Betty, my friend from up the street, or Ivan, my son-in-law, because they usually came to my back door when they visited.

I heard the two women trashing my place for quite awhile, and I was afraid to open the bathroom door. I discovered later that they dumped all of my drawers and stole anything that looked valuable. They found my pistol, and I'm glad they didn't use it. Later the police recovered it. They took my silverware, my purse, and my car and ran up some charges with my credit cards.

I have never heard a voice so welcome as my friend Betty when she called to me at my little bathroom window. She had felt strongly compelled to come over after not being able to reach me on the telephone, even though she knew I was having dinner with my family. God had answered my prayer! I was thankful to him for all the help he gave me throughout this harrowing ordeal.

Betty got me outside into the fresh air. My shirt was so bloody the ambulance driver told her to get me another one, which she did. The neighbor called the ambulance. The hospital stitched up my face and tried to clean the awful fire extinguisher stuff off of me, but they didn't do a very good job. My daughter did much better when she got me home and into the shower.

Thankfully, the police quickly captured the two women. The judge sentenced them each to twenty years in prison. Later that year the pregnant woman gave birth to a baby daughter, but tragically she was drug damaged and only lived a short time.

I'm grateful that there was insurance to cover the damages to my property. Almost everything in my home had to be replaced. The chemical sprays even ruined my kitchen stove. My daughter and her husband took me into their home for several months while my home was repaired, and I recovered physically and emotionally from the violent attack and robbery. I'm glad I could eventually move back into my home. They did such a good job on the renovation. I'm glad to be here in more ways than one!

Lost and Found

by
Pastor Chris Breuninger

In 1978, the year I graduated from high school, marijuana use was at an all-time high, and I was caught up in that hazy cloud. I began experimenting with drugs at age fourteen as a way of fitting in, and by the age of sixteen, I was both dazed and confused. My teenage years were toxic.

My parents were understandably frustrated. They had experienced a spiritual awakening, and they wanted me to know their joy. As good parents, they loved me in spite of my risk-taking stupidity, confronted me about my self-destructive behavior, and, most importantly, they prayed. They met with other parents of prodigal sons and daughters, and together they prayed that God would pursue their lost loved ones. Their prayers made my life a living hell. Because of their prayers, I began to reluctantly appreciate a spiritual reality that I was not interested in acknowledging. Furthermore, the partying life that had fostered a superficial happiness now began to look and feel empty. I began to get an unsettling sense that God may be real, and that this God was after me.

As I had done for years, I tried running away by piling distraction upon distraction and by continuing to live the party life in spite of its diminishing return of satisfaction and its increasing levels of emptiness. As I began my first year of college, and another year of partying, the emptiness grew louder. After a night of partying, I stumbled to my dorm room, crawled into bed, turned off the light, looked up at the ceiling, and wondered, "Surely there has got to be more to life that all this." Little did I know that God was beginning to orchestrate a major move in my life, and the frustration and emptiness that God was stirring in me was just the warm-up.

Back at my parent's church, Newport Covenant Church, a group of young adults had just returned from a yearlong session at a Bible School in Sweden. This experience had been transformational for them, and it gave my parents an idea. In the past, their attempts to introduce me to spiritual things had been meet with a cold shoulder and an indifferent yawn. I just didn't care about God; I was having too much fun, or so I thought. Now my parents had a hook—Europe. After I returned for a mid-term break, they offered me a deal. "Attend this Bible School in Europe for a year," said my Dad, "and we'll pay for your tuition if you pay for your airline ticket and other travel." I know my Dad mentioned Bible School, but I didn't hear that. All I heard was Europe. All I thought about was drinking German dark beer, skiing in the Alps, and meeting Danish Women. Thankfully, God would use my misdirected desires to lead me to my true desire.

The application I had to fill out to apply for the Bible School was a challenge. "Describe why you want to attend this school," read the application. "A multicultural experience would be beneficial to me," I wrote, without much conviction. Another question asked me to describe my Christian Faith. "I am unsure about my faith at this time," I wrote honestly, "but I am interested in what the Bible has to say about a Philosophy for life," which was partially true. After all, I had read some of the Bible, but it seemed remote and irrelevant. On the other hand, there was one book of the Bible that rang true to me. The Book of Ecclesiastes' reflections about the vanity and meaninglessness of life seemed real enough. But I had little hope that the words of a confused pagan would be taken seriously by the religious leaders of a Bible School.

A week later, I was back at Western Washington University to finish off my first year of college. One day, while poking around a used record shop, the women behind the counter, whom I knew, said, "Hey, Chris. I know you like the Clash and KZOK is sponsoring a contest in their name. Check it out." She handed me about two hundred entry forms, saying, "Give some to your friends." I put the forms in my backpack, rode my ten-speed back to my dorm, put the entry forms in my desk drawer, and forgot all about them. On a rainy day a few weeks later I opened my desk drawer, took out the forms, and filled-out all two hundred of them. I did not entertain much hope of winning, since I had never won anything before, but I had nothing better to do on a gray winter day. On the last form, I noticed that the contest was called "London Calling," the title song of my favorite Clash album. With that song on my lips, I rode back to the store, dropped off the forms, and thought nothing more about them.

Three weeks later as school was winding down, I received a letter from Cappenwray, a Bible School in Sweden. I opened the letter wondering how they might have composed their rejection, and I was surprised and confused, as I read that they had accepted me. Could this be right? Did they have the right guy? I looked at the envelope, and at the addressee, and sure enough, they were writing to me. A sinking feeling began to settle in my stomach, as I wondered whether God might have something to do with this arrangement.

After I received my letter of acceptance, I began to feel like God was haunting me. The more I felt God's pursuit, the faster I tried to run away. While driving one day, I ran a red light turning left, and nicked a car, bumper to bumper. The hit was so light that no impact was felt, but the sound of the bumpers hitting, rang like a bell inside my car. I pulled over to the side of the road, shaking from a near catastrophe, and sensed God saying in this miraculous moment, "You can run, but I can run faster."

During that summer, I did little to earn the money I would need for travel to Europe. Not earning money was one more way for me to avoid God. But God would not be deterred so easily. On a summer day, with just weeks before I was to return to Western Washington University, I received a phone call from the radio station. "Congratulations, Chris. You're our grand-prize winner, and you've just won a round trip to London England." I almost dropped the receiver. That sinking feeling was back. I began to realize that God's pursuit was more persistent that I had imagined.

My application should have been rejected by any rational criteria. I did not earn money to pay for my travel or for an airline ticket. As Western began its term, I was on a 747, traveling to Sweden to attend, of all things, a Bible School. On the flight, I remember thinking two conflicting thoughts: "OK, maybe I'll get this God thing worked out, and, along the way, maybe I'll stop at Amsterdam to buy some hash."

After I arrived at the Bible school, I wondered how long I would last. The students seemed happy, and their joy made me feel miserable. Their enjoyment of life without any toxins contributed to my gloom. To further my misery, the school scheduled five hours of Bible teaching each day. Five hours! What was I doing here? To dull this depressing reality, I spent the afternoons smoking pot in the forest with three fellow students. I left my bags packed, convinced that I would not last two weeks in this place.

During the second week, a German teacher by the name of Christian Bastke arrived. His course was called "The Life and Ministry of Jesus." I knew nothing about Jesus. In my estimation, Jesus was just another wide-eyed, fanatical, religious teacher that his followers inflated after his death to keep the wheels of their religion greased. Mr. Bastke systematically dismantled my naive preconceptions by presenting the life of Jesus, the purpose of his visitation, the veracity of his miracles, the historical evidence for his resurrection, and how his life fulfilled God's purposes for creation. I was awestruck. I had never heard any of this before. My circuits were overloaded, and I knew I had reached a crossroads in my life.

During the second week of school, while smoking pot with classmates in the forest, I looked down at my bag of toxins, and realized that I was standing at a critical junction, and that the last barrier holding me back from God's claim on my life was that bag. I took the bag, crumpled its contents to the ground, dropped to my knees and said a very simple prayer. "God, I give up. I can't run any more. I'm out of gas. I surrender. I'm yours."

Conversion is always a miracle that is displayed in a billion different ways. For some, like the disciples, the miracle is a process of understanding, misunderstanding, clarifying, and learning to follow Jesus. For others, like Paul, it is a dramatic event. In every case, conversion is a miracle that gives witness to the weaving of his grace in our lives. My conversion to Jesus was an event of surrender. After years of running away, I ran out of steam, and finally turned to the God who had lovingly and faithfully pursued me.

After my conversion, God seemed to make up for my time away. I was hungry to learn and to grow, and God began opening doors. During that year, I was chosen to lead small group Bible studies and local outreach teams, first in Sweden, then, later, in London. My enjoyment of these ministries and the affirmation of others provided early confirmation of gifts for ministry, which were developed during an Internship at Newport Covenant Church and on staff at a campus ministry after I returned to Western Washington University. These early experiences cultivated a burning desire to devote my energies to full-time Kingdom service as a pastoral leader, which I have done in Chicago, Twisp and, now, at PLCC.

As you might guess, I can identify with Jesus' parable of the Prodigal Son. Like me, this prodigal wandered away, walked the wild side, came to his senses, and returned home expecting to be punished, but instead was welcomed with great joy. Like that prodigal, I was lost, but now am found, and I stand amazed at the miracle of God's forgiving grace. That miracle changed my life and continues to shape my ministry.

Having walked the wild side and having experienced deep darkness, I have a soft spot for those who walk in darkness. Having experienced the bright light of God's forgiving grace, I am compelled to share this good news with as many people as I can. Working to bring this good news to the very place where I raised so much hell in years past seems very redemptive to me. Lost and found. To God be all glory.

DIVINE HEALINGS

Jesus turned and saw her. "Take heart, daughter," he said, "your faith has healed you." And the woman was healed from that moment.

Matthew 9:22

Proof of the Miraculous

by
Holly Barlow

As I approached my fiftieth birthday, I started to suffer from anemia from heavy menstrual flow. Iron supplements helped a little, but couldn't keep up with the loss of blood. Then one day I woke up with a prolapsed uterus and made an immediate appointment to see my doctor. He told me that a hysterectomy would solve both of these problems, so he referred me to a gynecological surgeon. She agreed with the need for surgery, suggesting that she could do a less invasive procedure than full abdominal surgery. Unfortunately a routine, pre-operative ultrasound uncovered what she called a "seven centimeter, complex, blood-filled mass" the size of a small orange on one of my ovaries. She assured me that it wasn't cancerous, but it did mean that I would have to have the abdominal procedure after all, removing my uterus and one ovary. She would leave the other one if it appeared normal.

As the day of the surgery approached, my friends from church began to pray for me and for my doctor. One day I noticed that my uterus no longer felt prolapsed. Had the mass gone down, no longer putting pressure on my uterus? A couple of days before the operation, I asked my doctor to do another ultrasound, just to make sure. She refused to do the test, telling me, "This is not a water-filled ovarian cyst that comes and goes. It is a complex, blood-filled, ovarian mass. These NEVER go away!"

When I awoke from sedation in my hospital room, my doctor came to see me and told me an incredible story: when she opened up my abdomen she found two perfectly healthy ovaries with no sign of that complex mass—not even a trace!

"Wow! Praise God! Thank you, Jesus!" These were my first thoughts on hearing about my miraculous healing. However, as I experienced the slow and painful recovery from the abdominal procedure, I started to have other thoughts. Without the mass, the surgeon could have done a simpler, less painful procedure. I wondered, "Why did you heal me, God, yet still put me through the ordeal of abdominal surgery? Was a healing even necessary, since the doctor would simply have removed the ovary anyway?"

I was grateful to be able to retain both ovaries, thus putting off menopause until I naturally go through it; but it didn't seem to warrant a miracle.

After six weeks, I visited the surgeon again, for a post-op visit. We discussed how my recovery was going and other health issues, and then I said, "We need to talk about that mass on my ovary." She told me that after she saw that it was gone with no trace, she contacted the radiologist who read the ultrasound, to double check his findings. He assured her that the mass had been very much real; it was not a diagnostic error.

The doctor told me she was amazed because, "these almost never go away."

"*ALMOST* never?" I replied. "Before the surgery you said NEVER."

"Well, that was before *yours* went away."

As I pressed her, she admitted, "It was like a miracle."

"*LIKE* a miracle?" I said.

"Ok, it WAS a miracle!"

I told her that a lot of people had been praying for me and that another woman in my church had had a similar complex mass, though smaller, resolve in the same way. She laughed and said, "TWO women? I have to start going to your church!"

Then she got serious and told me, "I'm going to practice medicine differently from now on. You told me before the surgery that you felt something had changed, but I refused to do the test. From now on I will be more open to what my patients tell me; to be willing to look for things I don't expect."

Now it became crystal clear to me why God had performed this healing miracle. It wasn't entirely for my benefit that I experience better health, but for the benefit of my doctor, that she would open her mind to God's healing power and perhaps open her heart as well. It reminded me of how Jesus often performed miracles for the purpose of authenticating his power and authority. That certainly was the case here.

As I look back on the unnecessarily complex surgery and painful recovery that I endured, I would willingly go through it again as a testimony to the power of God to heal and to save. Amen and Amen!

A Heartfelt Miracle

by
Ed Buffalow

Blue sky above and blue water below—I was a nine-year-old boy looking down at the far end of the swimming pool twenty-five yards away. It was a typical summer day for me at swim practice. But this day was to be the first of many terrifying episodes that were going to affect my life for decades to come.

The coach wanted us to swim the full length of the pool without taking a breath. As I dove into the cool water, I felt a funny sensation in my chest. My heart started pounding at a fast rate. I couldn't even think of the coach's instruction to hold our breath. With each stroke of the water, I was gasping for as much air as I could take in. I went to the side of the pool to rest, but my heart did not want to slow down. After practice, the coach came over and measured my heart rate with the familiar stopwatch hanging around his neck. His eyes bulged out as he did the math—over two hundred beats per minute!

This elevated heart rate continued all day. In the evening, our family doctor came to the house. They still did things like that in those days. He said my heart would settle down and assured us that this was something I would eventually out grow. It did finally settle down about 8 p.m. that night, but it was not something I would out grow.

In my adult years, these episodes would come on unexpectedly, usually at stressful and inconvenient times: on a backpack trip in the middle of the mountains after my wife Nancy had an accident, when we were shopping for a new car, when we had an open house for our newly completed home. These occurrences were painful and scary to endure.

In the summer of 1986, I was in the process of a job transition. We now had our first child, six-month old Christine. I was in the yard installing timber steps when my heart kicked into high gear. For some reason I became particularly anxious. Perhaps my heart would just get tired out and stop, I feared. Nancy called 911, and the arrival of sirens only increased my anxiety and heart rate all the more. I was rushed to the hospital and given medication to slow my heart down.

The next day, I was set up with a cardiologist appointment. He indicated that my condition was known as P.A.T. or Paroxysmal Atria Tachycardia. For those who do not know Greek, it basically means rapid heart rate. The doctor went on to explain that I had an inverted heart valve. He prescribed medication for me to take to curtail the episodes and to take immediately after an event to bring the heart rate back down. He also informed me that stress, alcohol and caffeine were not good for my condition.

Because of the diagnosis, I found myself in a very dark and fearful state. Here I was in my early thirties, starting a new job, paying off the mortgage of a new house with a new baby daughter. The alcohol and caffeine were easy to drop. But stress? How do you live life without stress? I became frozen in fear. At work, I avoided stressful assignments and meetings, as best I could. At home, I became withdrawn and isolated, not taking on any stressful activities.

I lived in this darkened state for a year until the fall of 1987, when the first ray of light illuminated some hope. Our Pastor at University Presbyterian Church, Bruce Larsen, returned from a study leave telling the congregation that God had directed him to do a year-long sermon series on the topic of FEAR. Are there times in your life when it seems that God has directed your pastor to give a sermon just for you? For me, this series seemed tailor made. Over the course of that year, I learned incredibly valuable information that I could apply directly to my life.

I had never been one to go for counseling, but at this point, I felt prompted to share with Pastor Larson my personal struggles with health fears. He gave me a simple powerful piece of advice that I have never forgotten, one that I continue to apply to my life and share with others. He asked me, "How are you doing right now?" I said,

"Fine." That was it in a nutshell. Too often, we live our lives in the unknown future, not enjoying the blessings of the present moment. Pastor Larson taught me to live in the present moment and enjoy the gift of God's grace. He also offered, "You know, once a month we have a healing service. No guarantees, but you might consider it."

The Healing Service at University Presbyterian Church was held on the last Sunday of each month. On October 25, 1987, I went. Many others in need of healing were in line with me. On the altar stage were several pairs of pastors and elders. When it was my turn, I explained my health condition and my fear to the pastor and elder I was assigned to. They anointed my head with oil and prayed for my healing.

That fall, I began an intense word study to see what the Bible had to say about fear and the heart. I came across many verses. My banner verse became Philippians 4:6–7 *"Do not be anxious about anything, but in everything, by prayer and petition, with thanksgiving, present your requests to God. And the peace of God which transcends all understanding, will guard your hearts and your minds in Christ Jesus."*

This word study led to an intense renewed interest in the Bible. From this point on, I became very involved in adult and men's ministries by facilitating, teaching and developing curriculum that continues fruitfully and joyfully to this day.

Through the struggles with my heart ailment, The Holy Spirit had energized me to a deeper level of spirituality. The dark clouds that had enveloped me for so long began to lift. The fears that had taken over my life subsided. I began to count the weeks, then the months and finally the years without a heart episode. Since that time, I have not had a single heart episode.

During a routine annual exam in my late forties, my family doctor wanted me to see a cardiologist for a more detailed EKG. I went back to the same cardiologist who had treated me earlier, but because it had been over seven years, he had no record of my prior visits. He concluded that I have a great heart—a strong and healthy one. He made no mention of an inverted heart valve. Over the past ten years I have had EKGs, Echo Cardiograms and heart scans. No abnormalities were found.

I believe that I was miraculously healed. I have had no heart episodes since 1987, although I had regular episodes from age nine to thirty-four. I am no longer living under a cloud of fear. I was ignited by the Holy Spirit to a deeper spiritual life that continues to this day. Was the healing due to my pastor's counseling? Was it my faith to go to the Healing Service or the healing prayers themselves? Was it the anointing of oil? Was it God's Word reviving my heart, mind, body and soul? Was it the blessing of the Holy Spirit? These are all questions I have pondered.

What I do know for certain is that for the past nineteen years I have not been plagued by the racing heart episodes and the associated fears, and I am remarkably closer to God than I was before. Thanks be to God.

The Miracle of April 25, 1945

by
Norman Cool

It was April 25, 1945. World War II, the deadliest war ever waged, was ending in Europe. On the home front in Whittier, California, the battle for the lives of my wife, Bertha, and our unborn child was just beginning.

Right after lunch that day, Bertha went into labor. We rushed to the hospital in our car, as there was no ambulance available to take us. At the emergency entrance, Bertha was put on a gurney and whisked to the delivery room. She was hemorrhaging badly and had already lost a frighteningly large amount of blood. I went the other direction to register her at the front desk. Afterwards I made my way to find Bertha. In those days, husbands typically weren't present in the delivery room during childbirth, but I was permitted to stand in the open doorway and watch the drama unfold.

I looked on nervously as the doctor and nurses diligently worked over Bertha, who was in the midst of an emergency cesarean section. Then Bertha's physician came down the hall and entered the room. I noticed that he stopped for a moment and bowed his head in prayer before taking his place at the operating table. The medical team was focused on Bertha, when her doctor's partner held up our little baby boy by the feet and said, "Well, that's that." A nurse took our lifeless son and put him on a cart with the used instruments. She pushed it out of the way, as the medical team continued to focus their efforts on Bertha. No one attended to our son. They just left him lying there alone, as they turned their full attention to my wife.

Naturally, Bertha was asking about the welfare of our baby. The Anesthetist explained to her that the baby had withstood incredible trauma during labor and delivery and had lost too much oxygen to the brain. He had not made it. He went on to say that it was a blessing because even if the baby had lived, he would have been severely brain-damaged because of the oxygen deprivation. Bertha, already quite weak from the trauma, went into shock from the tragic news of our son's death.

As the medical team focused all of their attention on saving Bertha's life, I watched a strange and miraculous event unfold before my eyes. A mysterious lady in a dark gray coat entered the delivery room from a back door. She looked at our lifeless baby lying alone on the cart, and then she quickly left the room. It occurred to me that she was not dressed in hospital garb like the rest of the medical team. She was wearing street clothes and looked like she had just come in from outside the building. It seemed odd to me at the time.

Just as quickly, as she had left the room, she returned with an oxygen tank. She put the mask over our baby's small face and within what seemed like seconds, our son began to cry. Then the mysterious woman took the oxygen tank and quickly left the room. No one looked up or paid any attention to her at all. It was as if I was the only one who could see her. The doctors and nurses seemed startled and amazed to hear our baby's cries. A nurse hurried to the abandoned cart, picked him up, and started to clean him.

This began the life of our son, David Cool. The doctors felt certain that he would be severely handicapped from the loss of oxygen to his brain during the traumatic birth, but miraculously he was perfectly fine and healthy. The doctors and nurses could not explain how the birth of our son had a happy ending that day, but we can. God had other plans for David's life. Of our two sons, David grew up to become the child who takes care of us now that we are in our nineties and can't get around as easily as we once could. God knew that our family needed David, and he saw to it that our son lived that fateful day in April 1945.

Second Chances and Miracles

by
Carla Trulson-Essenberg

"You have end-stage lung disease and your only option is a double lung transplant…your only option is a double lung transplant…your only option is a double lung transplant." These words kept echoing through my mind. I heard my doctor go on to say that I had a bacterium called Pseudomonas, which was overtaking my lungs. If I did not have this operation, I would die.

When I heard these words from my pulmonary doctor in November 2002, my first reaction was to think of my family. It was pity party time! Would I see our daughter Kirsten get married? Would I see our son Eric graduate from college? My pity party lasted but a few moments. My thoughts almost immediately turned to feelings of being so blessed to have a husband like Dave and so blessed to have children that know and love the Lord.

I have always had a deep faith. On that diagnosis day, I made a choice to trust in God. My touchstone Bible verse has always been Proverbs 3:5–6 *"Trust in the Lord with all your heart and lean not onto your own understanding; in all your ways acknowledge him, and he will make your paths straight."* On that day, I climbed into the palm of God's hand. Every nook and cranny in my body was filled with the Holy Spirit. I was flooded with an amazing peace, and from that point on, I experienced absolutely no fear. At that moment, I knew I was in the middle of God's will, and no matter what happened, I would always be in his presence.

From the very first days of my diagnosis, I was aware that someone would have to die in order for me to have a second chance at life. This became a constant reminder to me of God's beloved child, Jesus Christ, dying to give me eternal life. What a sacrifice! What hope God gave to me! This awareness of someone dying so I could live was amplified the closer I got to the transplant. I would pray that my potential donor was living a life filled with joy. I prayed for the donor's family and for the difficult decisions they would be making, and I prayed they would find hope and peace in the midst of their grief.

God let me know from the get-go that how I reacted to my diagnosis would affect how others would react. God gave me the wisdom and strength I needed to approach the journey ahead of me. To keep our lives as normal as possible for as long as possible, Dave and I initially chose not to say anything to anyone, except for a very few close friends.

In the months following my diagnosis, my life was filled with patience, joy, contentment, and an amazing peace. I had worked in the medical field most of my adult life, and I knew that what I would be going through was BIG. I knew I might not survive, but the thought of dying was not frightening at all. When we shared my diagnosis people would ask, "Are you afraid?" I would tell them that I was not afraid because God had given me this amazing peace. When people say, "You're such an inspiration!" I tell them, "It's a God thing. All the glory goes to God."

Backtracking a bit, when I was born at a small hospital in beautiful Northern Michigan, an accident caused me to inhale meconium. Shortly after my birth, I was taken downstate to another hospital, where I eventually coughed up a plug of this material; but the damage to the cilia in my lungs had already occurred. My lungs would constantly fill up with fluid, and as I grew older, this became more difficult to remove. I was very susceptible to colds, bronchitis and pneumonia and eventually developed bronchiectasis. I had most of my left lung removed after my first year of college. On the upside, my childhood was very happy with wonderful, supportive, Christian parents and six siblings whom I love dearly. I never thought of myself as a victim. It was important to me to "just be normal," which I felt I was.

Thanks to my upbringing, I nurtured my faith through prayer, Bible study, and regular worship at PLCC. At the end of January 2003, I contacted Linda Knodel, RN, in Parish Nursing at our church and confidentially shared my situation with her. She jumped into action and assured me that PLCC, the local body of Christ, would be there for whatever I needed. She put me in contact with Dr. Aye, a thoracic surgeon in our congregation, who prayed for me and shared information regarding transplants and surgeons. Over the next few weeks, I shared this news with my Bible study and other close friends in the church and community. Soon people all over the world were praying for me and supporting me in many ways.

I was referred to the University of Washington Medical Center in Seattle. This facility is the only hospital in a five state area (Washington, Alaska, Idaho, Oregon and Montana) authorized to do lung transplants. The United Network for Organ Sharing (UNOS) has divided the nation into regions, and the University of Washington Medical Center is in Region Six. They have been doing lung transplants since 1992. When they get a call from UNOS that there is a donor, they send a team of people to harvest the lungs, which have no more than a six-hour shelf life. The recipient is determined by blood type, lung size, and severity of illness. My blood type was A-negative. I was told that the average wait on the list was approximately nine months for someone of my blood type and lung size.

Sometime after I had been put on oxygen at night, I had my first Transplant Team consultation with Dr. Tonelli, a top-notch pulmonologist with a wonderful dry wit who specializes in people with bronchiectasis and cystic fibrosis. He likened me to the Sherpa guides in the Himalayans whose bodies have adapted to a very low amount of oxygen. Even though my oxygen saturation levels were very low, I could still function at a quite high level. A normal person would be panting for breath on the amount of oxygen I was taking in.

Soon I started jumping through the many hoops required to be considered a candidate for a transplant. The statistics for survival are about eighty percent at the end of one year and forty-seven at five years. As I was still feeling quite well, I made the decision to be put in a "holding pattern," holding off on the transplant as long as I safely could. Eventually I required oxygen full-time. I grew attached to my little Helios tank and would tote it around in purses or bags that I could sling over my shoulder.

The Transplant Team continued to monitor me. When I was hospitalized for a second time in June 2004 to have another peripherally inserted central catheter (PICC) line placed for self-administered infusions, I felt that God was telling me to go on the transplant list in October.

Key words for a transplant patient are "the list" and "the call." To get on "the list," one has to undergo very stringent testing of every system of the body to make sure there are no other conditions that would prevent one from being a candidate for a transplant. This regimen included psychological testing, meetings with social workers, dietitians, financial counselors, and twelve sessions of pulmonary rehabilitation with other potential transplants. Once on "the list," a patient is required to stay within three hours of the hospital at all times and to be available by pager or phone at all times for "the call." After surgery, one must stay within one hour of the hospital and have a caregiver 24/7 for three months.

Fast forward to Halloween 2004, which was a beautiful sunny Sunday morning. I had been on the waiting list for a double lung transplant for just five days. Dave and I were supposed to "greet" at the 10:30 a.m. church service that day. Dave said he would greet for both of us and asked me to go in and save him a seat. Dr. Aye saw me and came over to talk. He asked how I was doing and offered to pray with me. I asked for prayer for my future donor, the donor's family, the surgeon, the transplant team, and for my family.

Twenty minutes later, during the service, my beeper went off. Dave and I looked at each other with shock. Could this really be "the call?" We left the sanctuary, went to the narthex, and called the lung transplant coordinator at UWMC to see if it was a legitimate call. "Yes, we have a set of lungs for you. Please get here as soon as possible." I glanced back in the church, saw that Dr. Aye was participating on the Praise Team, and calmly asked the usher to tell Dr. Aye the news.

God continued to bestow that amazing peace on me. I have been more frightened going to the dentist than I was going to get my double lung transplant. As we quickly headed for home before leaving for the hospital, one of my thoughts was, "Oh, I didn't get my closets all cleaned!"

At the hospital they started prepping me for surgery about 1 p.m. Surgery began shortly after 4 p.m. I was wheeled into the

Recovery Room shortly after 11:30 p.m. I had just become the 284th lung transplant for the UWMC since 1992. When I eventually came out of my anesthesia stupor, Dave asked me what day it was. "Why, Sunday night, of course," I replied. "It's Thursday!" he said.

The remarkable thing was that when I awoke, and to this day, I had absolutely no pain from the incision site. I had a clamshell incision, which extended across the chest from one armpit to the other. My sternum had been broken and wired back together. When the ICU nurse asked if I wanted any pain medicine, I replied, "I have no pain." The doctor came in and asked, "Are you trying to tough it out?" But it was not a matter of toughing it out—I simply had no pain. The nurse kept saying, "It's a miracle!"

My stay in the hospital was one of ups and downs. I spent twenty-one days in ICU and a total of thirty-five days in the hospital. I was hooked up to many tubes and monitors. My body was massively swollen. I had no concept of time, as it was always light in ICU and there were always noises and beeps. Over the ensuing days, some tubes were taken out and others were put in. "Paddles" were used. Invasive procedures were performed. I hallucinated and even suffered a small stroke. I had to retrain my brain how to deep breathe and cough with my new lungs. The most important things during this time were the support of my family, which included my sister Monna flying in from Michigan for four weeks, and the prayers. I could feel them from all over the world. I was so grateful to God, my donor, my doctors, and the transplant team for this gift—this second chance at life here on earth. Golfers will appreciate that the name of my transplant surgeon is Dr. Mulligan. In golfing terminology, a "mulligan" is a second chance.

After returning home, PLCC, the local body of Christ, came through big time. Amy Quinn did a spectacular job of coordinating over thirty people for care giving. These people included members of PLCC, family from near and far, friends, neighbors, and members of our Bible study group. Caregivers were scheduled from 6:30 a.m. until 6:00 p.m. during the week, while Dave was working; many others sent or brought meals, cards and gifts. And those closets I was worried about when I got "the call" for transplant? They, along with my house, got cleaned during this time too.

The unsung heroes of this story are my immediate family, and I am so grateful for them. Every day for thirty years, Dave did percussion and postural drainage on me. Kirsten and Eric grew up thinking this was a normal thing. They told me later that for a long time they thought every Mom had to be percussed. It was never a big deal. We just did it and went on with our lives. I don't normally share this particular part of my life, but you need to know this so you can understand how different my life is today.

"Amazing" would be a good word to describe my second chance at life, this miracle. Every morning I awaken with joy, wonderment, and astonishment at how well I can breathe. I did not know that people breathed like this. I always thought one had to work at it. Now I have no congestion, no shortness of breath, no oxygen and probably most life changing of all—no more percussion and postural drainage. I feel better than I have ever felt in my life, even younger than I did when I was in high school. I can easily walk four to five miles a day and am able to do things that I could only dream of doing before.

Remember the pity party I had in November 2002, when I received my diagnosis? On June 10, 2006, God honored me with the opportunity of being there when our son Eric graduated from Western Washington University. Then on August 5, 2006, God again honored me with being able to see our daughter Kirsten marry the man of her dreams. I am so grateful to God for these gifts!

Why did God give me a second chance at life? I don't know the answer to that, but I do know that the Holy Spirit keeps nudging me to share both my story of faith and trust and to encourage others. I have started working with the Lung Transplant Support Group to do just that for those who are on this same journey as I.

The question I am most frequently asked is, "Do I know who my donor is?" The answer to that is, "No." Dr. Mulligan told me that the donor was a teenager to young adult. I wrote a letter to the family, but I have yet to hear back.

My body will always try to reject these lungs, so I will be on anti-rejection medications the rest of my life. I have some side effects which include: a suppressed immune system, slight hand tremors, leg weakness, weight gain, loss of my hair (it's growing back), and some difficulty focusing; but these seem so insignificant. Every day is so precious to me. If I were asked to give advice, it would be to live each day as if it were your last. Eliminate "someday" from your vocabulary. As my friend, Molly, says, "Don't go to work on Monday and wish it were Friday." Get connected to others in your church, be part of a small group, and practice hospitality by inviting others into your home.

Remember, have faith, then trust, and joy will follow. That is not to say you will have no suffering. However, you can be sure that when that dark cloud enters your life, God will come into the middle of that cloud and be with you.

God was with me throughout this journey, and I feel so privileged to have experienced it. If I could turn back the hands of time, I would not change a thing in my life. In Ephesians 3:20–21 the Bible talks about how God is able to do immeasurably more than all we ask and imagine and that all glory for this goes to God. In my growing-up years and through the years that followed, I never thought to ask, nor did I even imagine, the possibility that God would provide me with new lungs, a procedure that had not even been perfected a mere twenty years ago. Yes, I do give all the glory to God.

I am so grateful for this second chance to enjoy the miracle God has given me—the gift of life. God not only gave me the miracle of new lungs, but also amazing peace, guidance, perfect timing, absence of pain from the incision site, the ability to breathe like never before, and last, but not least, the miracle of prayers and support from so many people throughout this whole journey.

So, when you see me, don't *just* think of me as a person with a double lung transplant; think of me as one of God's miracles.

Renewed by Prayer

by
Dr. Ralph Aye

While attending the first evening of our opening weekend seminar on healing prayer at PLCC, the speaker, after leading us through scripture after scripture proclaiming God's truth about his healing power and his desire to make us whole, asked us all to finish the evening by praying silently about a need that we had. I'd been struggling for some time with moderately annoying and progressive pain in both shoulders, and had already had one injected twice. The pain began to limit some of my activities, and medically was beginning to head in the wrong direction. Still, I didn't consider it a very serious matter.

That night though, I felt compelled to pray for healing. Although I experienced nothing at the time, the next morning the pain was completely gone, together with any aches and pains I had elsewhere. It's been many months since then, and my shoulders remain symptom-free. As a medical professional, I have absolutely no explanation for it. As a Christian, I believe that prayer and the powerful words of truth that preceded them ushered me briefly into God's Kingdom, where his rules, rather than earthly ones apply, and my shoulders were made new. Praise to the Lord, who hears our prayers and heals us!

Healed by His Love

by
Carra Lee Bolger

I have known the power of prayer and healing from the Lord ever since I was a little girl growing up in Fairbanks, Alaska. I remember praying to him and asking him to heal me. One time when my dad was twirling me around in fun, he accidentally dropped me. The fall caused me to bite a hole in my cheek. My dad took me to the dentist right away. I remember sitting in the dentist's chair, as he examined my injured cheek. He said that milkshakes were all I could eat and drink until it healed in a few weeks. That night I prayed myself to sleep asking God to heal me. The very next morning I awoke to find that the hole in my cheek was miraculously gone.

The most dramatic healing I experienced from the Lord came much later in my life. In 1994, I was diagnosed with breast cancer. I was horrified to learn that the cancer had spread to my lymphatic system and five out of twenty of my lymph nodes were malignant.

I called a dear Christian friend for support. She was a real prayer warrior, and I knew I could count on her during this scary and difficult time. She immediately began praying "The Curse of the Fig Tree" over my breast cancer. It is a Bible story about Jesus found in the Book of Matthew 21:18:22. *Early in the morning, as he was on his way back to the city, he was hungry. Seeing a fig tree by the road, he went up to it but found nothing on it except leaves. Then he said to it, "May you never bear fruit again!" Immediately the tree withered.*

When the disciples saw this, they were amazed. "How did the fig tree wither so quickly?" they asked. Jesus replied, "I tell you the truth, if you have faith and do not doubt, not only can you do what was done to the fig tree, but also you can say to this mountain, 'Go, throw yourself into the sea,' and it will be done. If you believe, you will receive whatever you ask for in prayer."

My friend cursed my cancer to the root. She prayerfully asked that my cancer would shrivel, die, and never bear fruit again. As she prayed for me, I could feel the anointing of the Holy Spirit flow through me from the top of my head to my toes. She encouraged me to sing God's praises and be in his word all day long. She knew from God that I was healed. By his word, I was miraculously healed!

From that moment on, I felt God's presence and heard him say, "Carra Lee, I want you to know that you do not need chemotherapy." This was thrilling to me, as I did not want to have chemotherapy, even though all of the oncologists that I had consulted to date had told me that I needed radical treatments for my disease, both before and after any surgery.

Chemotherapy would mean that I would lose all my hair and most likely get very sick from the treatment. My husband Tom was scared. He wanted me to listen to the doctor's advice, since chemotherapy was a standard treatment for breast cancer. In my heart, I felt very conflicted. On the one hand, I wanted to get the best medical care available to treat my illness, and on the other, I wanted to be obedient to God. At a follow-up doctor's appointment, I told my breast specialist that I believed that God had healed me from any disease. While he listened patiently, ultimately he advised me to go forward with a mastectomy to be on the safe side. Tom and I were devastated by the news.

That day Tom asked me, "If you believe that God has healed you and you believe that he told you that you don't need chemotherapy, why hasn't God told you that you don't need a mastectomy?" It was a legitimate question, so I turned to the Lord in prayer. I distinctly heard God say that the mastectomy operation would be to his glory.

I wept before the operation. I didn't want to lose my breast when I knew that I was already healed, but I wanted to bring glory to God. What a horrible state to be in! I put my faith and life in the hands of the Lord, as I was wheeled into surgery.

Amazingly, coming out of the anesthesia, I literally felt God's love being poured into me, like a vessel being filled to overflowing by the power of his Holy Spirit. It was the most amazing experience I have ever had in my entire life. To this day, I find it very difficult to express in finite human terms the meaningfulness of what God did for me. All I know is that it truly was a divine experience. God's love flowed through me and poured out of me to everyone who I saw at the hospital that day, especially to Tom, who had been so anxious and caring for my well-being. Instead of feeling groggy and sad from the loss of my breast, I felt exhilarated, full of love, peace and joy. I had a oneness with my Lord that I had never experienced before. Through this significant event, the meaning of Romans 5:5 came alive to me, *"And hope does not disappoint us, because God has poured out his love into our hearts by the Holy Spirit, whom he has given us."* It was God's gift to me, which I have grown to appreciate more and more as the years have gone by.

A couple hours later, another amazing thing happened. God confirmed to me what he had said through a nurse friend from Evergreen Hospice. She came to the hospital to see me and repeated the exact same words that God had spoken a month earlier, "Carra Lee, I want you to know that you do not need chemotherapy." She later directed me to an oncologist who treated me with immunotherapy. He strengthened my immune system, instead of destroying it with chemotherapy and radiation.

The day after the surgery, my doctor gave me the results of the pathology report. There was not a trace of cancer in my breast tissue. I was not surprised. As I had known from the moment my friend had prayed for me over the phone, God had indeed healed me. I knew I did not need the mastectomy, but I wanted to bring glory to him through the confirmation of my healing.

God, my heavenly Father and my Lord Jesus, carried me through the rest of this most blessed year. Leaning on him throughout this experience brought me into a closer walk with him. *Great is Thy Faithfulness* became my personal anthem. I praise God for what he has done for me. God is sovereign.

Asked of God

by
Molly Baker

In 1993 after a failed marriage, I decided it was time to figure out who God was and how he fit into my life. I started attending Sunday services at PLCC and soon became hungry to know more about God. I also began attending a Bible Study on the Ten Commandments. I was so impressed that God drew me to the perfect study—seeing that I couldn't name one of the commandments, let alone all ten! This Bible study and another one on the Book of James helped me to accept Jesus Christ as my Lord and Savior. After this, everything changed for me.

My boyfriend Marlin and I had been dating for a couple of years. During that time, God showed me that I needed to put God first and grow in my faith, before I committed myself to another person. Marlin and I realized that our relationship was struggling because we were on very different journeys in our faith. We decided to stop seeing each other and trust that God would work out the timing and the details for us to be together.

I was baptized at Westminster Chapel in Bellevue, Washington in 1996. Then in 1997, God brought Marlin back into my life. We were married in 1999. God brought us back to PLCC as a couple in 2001, and we soon became members. We attended a marriage seminar at Rainbow Lodge, which was instrumental in providing a strong foundation for our marriage. Next, I took a spiritual gifts class where

I learned that my gifts were exhortation, administration, and teaching. I also got involved in women's ministries. During that time, we were thankful that our church family came along side us in prayer as we struggled to get pregnant for over two years.

In April 2003, our prayers were answered when our son was born. We chose the name, Samuel, because it means *asked of God*. This was a time of great celebration and change in my life. Becoming a mother was much harder than I had ever anticipated. I found myself very depressed, questioning myself, my faith and isolating myself from others.

Marlin and I started attending the Wednesday night trek at church entitled, *Lead like Jesus*. The course promised to transform our heart, head, hands and habits. For the majority of this ongoing study, I struggled immensely. It wasn't long into the course that I realized I didn't want to be transformed. I had fallen out of the habit of spending regular time with the Lord, and this study was pushing all my buttons.

My low point came in February 2004, when I admitted that what I really wanted to do was go to sleep and never wake up. For someone who had always been an upbeat and energetic person, this was a particularly hard truth to face. I began seeing a Christian counselor provided by the church who helped me to admit to myself and to others that I wasn't doing well. I needed help and that was OK.

The yearly church women's retreat was coming up in April, and I had no intensions of going. About two weeks before the retreat, the Lord showed me through the kind words of a friend that I needed to attend. In obedience, I went. While there, God also prompted me to sign up to be prayed for, which I did. That experience was incredibly powerful. At the appointed time, two women, including Pastor Tamara, were in the room with me. First, they anointed me with oil and asked me how they could pray for me. I told them briefly what I was struggling with and they began to pray, as if they knew my whole life story. Amazingly, they prayed for details that I had not even mentioned that I was struggling with. It was incredible how the Holy Spirit guided them. I remember Pastor Tamara clapping her hands together to make a very loud noise that even startled me, as she told the enemy that he wasn't welcome to torment me any longer. She ordered him to depart immediately in the name of Jesus Christ. At that very moment, I felt the burden of the depression I had been carrying being lifted from me, and I began to see myself as God sees me, as his beloved child. I was miraculously transformed.

Not long after this, I was asked if I was interested in being the coordinator of the MOPS Program (Mothers of Preschoolers) in the fall. I remember laughing out loud at the thought. Then I laughed even harder when God prompted me to teach on the subject of the *Daily Habits of Leading Like Jesus* at a Christian Youth Summit. During this time, I kept hearing God asking me when I was going to trust him and use the gifts he had given me. He kept saying, "I have given you everything you need by my divine power. Trust me." Not long afterwards, I went forward in faith and accepted the MOPS coordinator position. It was a challenging and rewarding experience.

What I find truly amazing in my spiritual journey is that God not only knew the depths of my struggles, he gave me opportunities to serve in the areas where I had struggled the most—being a mom and my daily habits. He impressed upon me the realization that without these struggles, I would not have been equipped to serve in these areas and help others. He also showed me that spending time with him on a daily basis was not optional in my life. I find that I need this time with the Lord to avoid becoming ineffective and unproductive in the knowledge of who God is and where I fit into his perfect plan.

Protected by Prayer

by
Flora Witten

My earliest memory growing up on the island of Java in Indonesia was being with a very gentle woman; unfortunately, she had just kidnapped me. I was four years old, and I was at the market with my mom and my nanny. My abduction must have happened quickly. The police told my mother that there was nothing they could do to recover me; their resources were extremely limited. Later, my mother told me how much she had prayed for my well being during that terrifying ordeal.

I remember walking and walking that day holding the woman's hand. It has been fifty-two years since the kidnapping, but it seems like just yesterday. If it were not for one police officer who saw me with her later that day and instinctively knew that I didn't belong with her, I wouldn't have made it home to the safety of my family that day or possibly ever. I'm grateful that the woman didn't hurt me and that my future wasn't in the hands of a stranger who would steal a child.

This wasn't the only time in my life that God protected me. When I was eight years old, living in Montreal, Canada, I was with some friends at a lake. It was decided that a group of adults would swim across the lake. They said I could go with them, as long as I wore plastic swimming tube around my waist.

A few minutes into the swim, I remember slipping out of my tube. I felt no fear because as soon as I sunk under the water, I saw a vision of a beautiful garden. There were gorgeous plants all around me and symphonic-like music playing in the air. I felt an incredible sense of peace and tranquility. I don't recall struggling to breathe. Again, it seems like it just happened, even though forty-eight years have gone by.

I was enjoying the peace of the garden so much. When I woke up on shore being resuscitated, I remember feeling angry that I was pulled away from that beautiful, spiritual place. I could listen to that music forever. I just wanted to stay in the garden, but clearly, God had other plans for my life. Thankfully, I wasn't traumatized by this experience. I later swam with a synchronized swim team and became a lifeguard.

I continued to have a strong yearning to go back to that garden. So much so, that I was often looking for ways to recreate that amazing feeling. I considered trying hallucinogenic drugs when I was a teenager in the 1960's. I even went so far as to tell my mom that I would be using drugs. I remember her replying, "All I can do for you now is pray." She did pray quietly, but fervently. Her prayers were answered because incredibly, I couldn't find any drugs. Again, God was faithfully protecting me, even though I didn't realize it at the time.

In my twenties, I was still trying to figure out who God really was. While my mother was a Christian, my father was a devout Jewish man. I was struggling to find some middle ground, and I didn't understand about the power of prayer.

When I was twenty-seven, I was hospitalized for ten days in intensive care in Mountain View, California with severe asthma. Even though I wasn't permitted to have visitors, somehow my friend, Carol, came to my side. I remember feeling sorry for her that she had to look at me with my blue fingertips and blue lips due to the low level of oxygen in my blood. I had just had a rather painful test that showed drastically low levels that made my condition critical. Carol asked if she could pray for me. I said yes because I wanted her to feel better, not because I thought it would help.

After Carol finished praying, miraculously I was better and immediately looked healthy again. My doctor requested a repeat of the test. He was stunned to find out that my oxygen levels were much better than normal. I recall him saying, "You now have the oxygen level of an Olympic athlete." I was still confused about what had just happened. I felt I should tell my doctor that my friend had just prayed for me. He didn't tell me whether he was a believer or not, but he did say that it wasn't medicine that had cured me.

I thanked Carol for her prayers. That's when she told me that it was God who had healed me, not her. I still didn't understand what was going on.

A few years later, Carol invited me to a three day Billy Graham Crusade in San Jose, California. On the third day while sitting in the bleachers with Carol and her husband, Ed, I *finally* understood who God is! I accepted Jesus into my life that day on October 1, 1981. I clearly saw how Carol's prayers were answered in the hospital when I was so ill.

Later in my life when more prayers were answered, such as when my father accepted Jesus, I again saw the power of God and the Holy Spirit at work. As recently as March 2006, the Lord once again protected me, when I was suddenly hospitalized and needed life saving surgery. I thought I might die and was surprised that I felt such peace.

The friend from PLCC who had taken me to all my medical appointments that day prayed with me at one of the doctor's offices. I will always remember that wonderful and tender prayer. Many others came forward during this time to pray and to take care of me. Again, God chose to spare my life by protecting me once more. I know that he has a plan for me, and I am feeling more and more each day that every breath I take is a gift from God—a miracle.

I am very grateful that through these miracles in my life, God has deepened my faith. He has taken me to a new level in my spiritual journey where I strongly sense that I need to be praying about what God wants me to do with the rest of my life!

DIVINE DIRECTION

He guides me in paths of righteousness for his name's sake.

Psalm 23:3

A Surprising Call

by
Terri Doull

When I was seventeen, I longed to know what God wanted to do with my life. About five years previously, I had asked Jesus into my life at summer camp. The pastor told all of us that God had a plan for each one of our lives. It was very good news to me, but what exactly was that plan? I prayed often that the Lord would let me in on this information, so I would know where to attend college. I was able to trust him enough to tell the Lord that I would do whatever he indicated.

One day in our living room, I heard a clear voice say, "I want you to be a nurse." It was so audible that I turned to look around for the source. Once again, I heard, "Be a nurse." Then instantly I knew the source. It was a little stunning. I remember thinking, "Really," and then perhaps a bit dubiously, "OK."

This was an interesting turn in my life, as it had never, ever, occurred to me that nursing would be a profession that I would be called to. A few summers before, my mother had signed me up as a "Candy-Striper" hospital volunteer, but I never saw any sick or injured patients. Instead, I was assigned to Central Supply, where my job was to wrap instruments for sterilization in the autoclave. It was boring to say the least.

I was accepted at the University Of Washington School Of Nursing, after completing the pre-requisites courses. Organic and inorganic chemistry and microbiology were not right up my alley, to say the least! The classes I had enjoyed the most in school had been English, music, and art. I persevered simply out of obedience to that clear calling, which I could no more deny than my own mother's voice.

Early on, I must have amused some of the clinical instructors with my obvious embarrassment at having to delve into such personal territory of my patient's lives like giving baths, and taking health histories. I had never been a patient myself, much less seen a dead body, so I was quite anxious about cadaver lab. It was not long before I strongly sensed Jesus Christ's presence beside me in those places where I did not really want to go. That was so encouraging, and each experience built courage for the next. It was clear to me that I was not alone in this journey at all.

While wearing my "nursing shoes" over the past thirty-some years, I have learned so much about people, about suffering and comfort, and about God's presence with his people. What a rich journey it has been. I find it hard to imagine a different life now.

For a long time, I didn't tell anyone about God speaking so clearly to me because it was so private, and I feared that someone might mock those very important words given to me. It was a great gift to receive, that undeniable leading that kept me from giving up when it was difficult and took me on a path I never otherwise would have traveled.

The Lord's firmness and kindness to me make me thankful over and over again, especially his promises to always be with me in that vocation and adventure he called me to. We're still on the adventure together! I am reminded of a Bible verse from Joshua 1:9 *"Have I not commanded you? Be strong and courageous. Do not be terrified; do not be discouraged, for the Lord your God will be with you wherever you go."*

Fields of Kindling and the River of Life

by
Helen Boyer

It was January of 2006. My marriage was coming apart. I had an image in prayer of my marriage relationship as a vast field of splintered fragments of bone dry white kindling—a million small deaths. Each shard was a misunderstanding, a barbed remark, an unreconciled dispute, an untended wound, or a bit of unresolved anger. I had been wandering in this vast dry desert for years, stumbling over the brokenness and shifting through the sharp, splintered, driftwood bits of the relationship—the debris of a relationship that had been broken and had drifted apart. I had lost the path God intended for me in this marriage. I could not see any path at all.

When I focused on this image, however, I could see, below the dead white splintered fragments, coppery orange shimmers of running water. I could see something that was sparkling and refreshing, golden and glinting.

Then one day as I prayed, these words came to me:

Reach for healing.
Reach for love.
Stay with the lifespring.

I realized that I needed to find the lifespring of love beneath the splintered fragments, the sparkling shining glint of love, deep beneath the tossed dry kindling. I was to reach for that lifespring, with every word I said. It was not a time to make points, to teach, or to lecture. It was a time to live together, to wash away the pain, to find a connection to the beginning that was love. At the beginning, there was love.

In a prayer, I was told, "You cannot direct events now. It is not yours to change the heart of another. Let the path unfold before you. God will lead you now. Hide nothing. Be open. You have nothing to fear. Restore your soul in this process. Let your soul be at rest. Do not resist, do not command or reject. Let the path be only one of love."

Around this time, I had a meeting with Pastor Tamara Buchan in which she pointed me to Ezekiel 37, the Old Testament story about the Valley of the Dry Bones. Her pointing this story out was striking to me because I had not described my fields of kindling image to her, and the stark desolate image of the Valley of Dry Bones was so similar. The sorrow of lost hope in that story was exactly how I felt. I knew the river of life was down below. But I did not see a way to get to the water through the fields of bone dry white kindling.

A couple of months later, on an early spring afternoon, I had an hour open up unexpectedly. I decided to take a walk. I was not at home but was in a part of town with which I was not very familiar. So I wandered, letting God lead me, and I found myself along the banks of Issaquah Creek. I got to a place where I instinctively went down to the water. The spring sun was shining on the clean rocks in the shallow riverbed. And then I saw it—the orange and coppery rocks and the golden sparkling light on running water, exactly as it had been in my vision of what was so far below the dry driftwood kindling, in my time of isolation from God in my marriage relationship. Here was the river of life, open and unencumbered. I had been led to it. God had laid the vision of hope that I had seen in prayer, at my feet in this world. As I stood by the creekside feeling grateful and awestruck, I understood God was saying to me, "Here is my living water, here for you anytime you need it. Use it. Refresh your soul."

I stayed with the knowledge that the flowing water was available to me at all times. Things got better. Gradually the heavy image of dry kindling faded away and the gentle image of living water became more present in my life and in my interactions with everyone, including my husband. Our marriage was not restored, but things did improve between us, and God's peace was evident in our separation process; we had no significant disagreements at that time. Years of counseling and effort and discussions had not brought about that miracle. God brought it about by physically walking me to the awareness of his living, revitalizing well of love.

In the Lord's Lap

by
Judy Aasheim

My husband and I were living in Holland when our first child, Gregory, was born during the Christmas season. When we lived in Belgium eighteen months later, our second son, Jeffrey, was born. Those were the years when I was beginning my serious walk with the Lord, teaching everything I learned to my little boys.

The day we said good-bye to our Belgian house, Gregory, who was almost four, sat on my lap and told me that he wished he could sit on Jesus' lap. Little did I know that within a few days his wish would become a reality.

During the week of our move, I was given knowledge by God that something was going to happen to Gregory, but not to Jeffrey. This would put any mother on high alert, yet I didn't feel any fear. I just mentioned it casually to my best friend the hour we departed and started our weeklong drive from Belgium to Geneva, Switzerland, our next assignment.

On September 16 of that year, we arrived at Lake Geneva and began hunting for a parking place near the park so we could have a picnic lunch, before going to our new home. As I turned to catch up with my husband and two little boys who were already crossing the busy street by the lake, I witnessed my calm, obedient, loving, little boy get hit by a car. Immediately, I knew what God had been preparing me for—the death of my beloved little boy, Gregory.

The only people we knew in Geneva were my husband's new boss and his wife, Bill and Judy. Their daughters were both Christians, but they resisted and continued viewing their daughters' faith with intellectual skepticism. Yet, Judy would one day tell me that when she and I were hugging in prayer for Gregory in the hospital following the accident, she felt a strange power emanating from my whole body. God used this tragedy to draw her to him.

As Gregory's prognosis looked grim, God continued preparing me for the inevitable. Just before the doctors came out to announce his death, I told Judy that I knew that Gregory had just died. Yet another example of how the Lord held onto me during this horrific time.

Naturally, the horror of witnessing your little one hit by a car is unbearable. I couldn't get the heartbreaking images out of my mind. The accident kept replaying repeatedly in my mind, threatening to drive me crazy. Thankfully, a group of Christians, who happened to be there at the time, prayed for me. Miraculously, the recurring images were transformed. I still knew full well what had happened to Gregory, but a blessed veil descended over it all, which acted like an emotional Novocain. Without it, I don't know how I would have gotten through the loss of my precious son.

God's Plan for Change

by
Kent T. Kiernan

When I was a patrol sergeant for nearly two decades in law enforcement, I put myself down like no lieutenant or captain ever did. After I left the force in 1999, I took one month off from any productive activity. I was physically sick and tired. My body went into rebellion, and I struggled to learn how to sleep and live a "normal" lifestyle. I began to face the painful emotions that I had "shoved down" for so long from the critical and traumatic situations that I had experienced during my law enforcement career. I had mistakenly thought that I had worked through them, but realized I was beating myself up from the inside out.

During this time, I found myself going through a grieving process of loss similar to the feelings that I had experienced when my dad had died. My thoughts and feelings fluctuated from wishing I had thanked those who had helped me along life's path to a scary sense of doubt in my self-worth as a man.

Fortunately, for those around me, I enrolled in a transformational personal training academy that helped me to see that the uniform I once wore was not all I was called to be. I knew that God was still holding on to me, even though I had walked away from my life of forty-six years in Utah to start over.

I scrutinized my life trying to determine the things I could change, and what I could throw out. One night I had a dream that gave me insight into my emotional struggles and helped me immensely. I was on a ship dock dragging a large rope with several boxes behind me. The boxes were in different shapes and sizes, some broken and worn, others new and unused. In the dream, it was crystal clear to me that the boxes represented relationships in my life. When I woke up, I was immediately able to release some of the old emotional baggage that I didn't need to take on this new journey. I went straight down to my basement and threw out two truckloads of old boxes that represented the past. Afterwards, I felt such a sense of newfound direction and purpose; my spirit came alive. Then I sat down, wrote letters to people that had hurt me, and burnt them in the fireplace.

I thought this new path I had discovered through the vivid dream was going to be easier and less stressful. Boy was I wrong! The ride I had embarked on was far bumpier and twisting than any Cedar Point roller coaster has to offer. I found myself more fearful than I had ever been in my life. I asked myself, "What the hell was I thinking when I packed my bags and left the life I had known for so long? What was drawing me out of my comfort zone?" Ironically, not knowing the answers to these questions was scarier than anything I had experienced as a cop. The bottom line was that I still had some very tough and deep emotional healing that needed to happen for me to move forward.

One of the emotions that I had buried was the ability to cry. I had been trained to handle situations in law enforcement that would make the average person cry their guts out. It was inevitable that overtime an emotional numbing of sorts had to take place in order for me to cope with the intense scenarios that I had grown accustomed to witnessing on the force. I started finding myself drawn to chick flicks, as an avenue to rekindle my sense of feeling in this area. My teenage daughters love kidding me, "Here he goes again! Throw him the box of Kleenex." How freed up I feel, as I continue to let go of the emotions that have been bottled up inside for so long.

Sometimes I feel like my life is similar to Job in the Old Testament except that he wasn't given the freedom to choose, as I have been. While I try to examine decisions from a godly perspective of service and compassion, I struggle to understand why I haven't yet found a career path that is more in line with how I see my giftedness. Having done much of the painstaking emotional work, I am now much more tuned into the realization that helping people energizes me.

I'm definitely seeking more balance in my relationships, as I feel that I treasure them more now than I ever did in the past. The Holy Spirit reminds me in subtle ways of people that were part of my life path that I never expressed my thanks to for giving their love to me. Sometimes I regret that some of these individuals have passed away and then feel guilt ridden in my heart. At those times, I turn to God in prayer, and it helps me understand his love even more.

For me, the miracle began with the dream and continues to unfold in my life, as I continue to seek out God's perfect will for my future. While I don't yet know exactly where God is leading me, I have put my faith in him trusting that his plans for me are far greater than anything I could envision for myself. My sincere prayer is that as I share this unfolding story in my spiritual journey, others will be able to move forward with faith in their lives as well. God bless you.

God's Miraculous "Move" in My Life

by
Pastor Tamara Buchan

L ife changed quite a bit for us as a family after 9/11 in 2001. At the time, my husband Bill and I were living in Denver, Colorado with our three daughters: Heather, Bonnie and Molly. Just days after it happened, we took Heather to college in Seattle at Seattle Pacific University (SPU). I remember President Bush declaring war on Afghanistan, while we drove Heather to spend her first night in the dorm. Bonnie and Molly also began attending their academic alternative school in a brand new building. The only downside was that it was thirty minutes away from our home. We decided to move out of our home of eleven years to be closer to their school and to Bill's job, which was an hour commute through Denver.

I was working closer to home leading, *The Journey Project*, which I started with a core group of about fifty other people the previous year. As I entered the Advent season, I decided that I wanted to fast and pray for God "to move powerfully in my life." I never dreamed just how faithfully and adventurously God would answer that prayer!

I will never forget the day. It was December 22, 2001, just three days before Christmas. I was hosting a brunch for a book study that I had been leading. During the brunch, I found out some wild things:

we received an offer to buy our house; the house we wanted to buy was purchased by another family; and finally the biggest news, Bill's company was being put up for sale. Needless to say, I was more than a bit distracted through the brunch.

We were disappointed about Bill's company being put up for sale. He was doing Risk Management and enjoying it very much. This company sale put us at job disruption number five, due to company buyouts.

The next day on December 23, Bill received a call from AT&T Wireless in Seattle asking him to interview. I remember the conversation so clearly. We were riding along after doing some Christmas shopping, and Bill told me that they wanted him to come to Seattle to interview after the holidays. I immediately knew in my spirit that he needed to go. We had never considered moving before; but with Heather already in school at SPU, it seemed like a door was already open in Seattle.

I realized that if AT&T Wireless offered Bill a job, it would mean laying down the ministry that I had given birth to and was leading. God miraculously gave me the courage to be able to do this. I had been asking God to "move" in my life, but I never dreamed he would answer us by literally "moving" us to Seattle.

We enjoyed a very special Christmas season. I went into the holiday knowing that it may be the last one that I would spend living close to my extended family. My parents also took our extended family to Mexico the day after Christmas to celebrate their fiftieth wedding anniversary. It felt bittersweet because I already knew deep down that we would be leaving.

We came home, and Bill went to interview for the position the second week of January 2002. They immediately offered him the job and asked us to move to Seattle. One of the first miracles of God's move in my life is how smoothly he worked out telling people. We started with our extended family. They were sad to see us go; but were delighted that if we had to move, it would be to someplace as sweet as Seattle. The next day I told the Conference Superintendent for Church Planting, who lives in Nebraska, but just happened to be in Denver. He actually cried along with me. The next night, I called a *Journey Project* gathering. I had a plan for how they could dismantle the ministry; but as I told them I was leaving, they said, "Tamara, you always said it wasn't about you, we still have important work to do." They continue to make an impact for Jesus in Denver and around the world through their projects.

After that emotional week, Bill left to go to Seattle, and I began the process of moving. The first sale of our house fell through, so we showed our house every day, sometimes more than once. This was challenging, as both Bill and I were working from home at that point. It was a hot real estate market, and houses were selling right away. For some reason that escaped us, ours continued to sit without a sold sign.

I came to Seattle in February on a house-hunting trip. We could have lived anywhere in the Eastside, but I felt led to the Plateau area in Sammamish. As we drove around, I would see PLCC, but never really got my bearings where it was. We probably looked at close to one hundred houses that week and finally decided to buy one of the last ones we toured. It was in the Troussachs development and had been on the market for nine months. Our realtor advised us to put in a low offer. One of the miracles of our move is that we didn't get that house. Another family offered more for it the same weekend. We tried to buy another house like it, but that one didn't work out either. God had a different plan for our location.

After I returned to Denver, I was pretty focused on finishing up my work with *The Journey Project* and getting us moved. As I thought about what I would do in Seattle, God gave me this huge peace that *he had important work for me to do.* I met with the Covenant Superintendent for the Midwest Conference who told me to contact the Superintendent in the North Pacific. He told me that there was only one position open—adult education and small groups at PLCC. I wasn't too interested in that job title, so I didn't pursue it. It wasn't until later that I found out the position included developing an equipping ministry, which is my biggest passion. Knowing that information changed my mind, and I told them that they could put my name into the mix. When I actually saw the job description, I said to myself, "This job was written just for me!" It was a perfect fit for my gifts and passions.

I made reservations to bring Bonnie and Molly out to Seattle in March so they would be convinced that it would be fun to move. Unfortunately, the weather on that trip was beyond miserable, along with Bonnie being quite sick. The good news is that they could help us look for houses because we hadn't seen anything we wanted to buy at that point. When we came to the house we currently live in, all three girls walked into the entry way and said in unison, "This is the house we are supposed to have!" Amazingly, within three hours we owned it. The fact that it was one of the first houses built in a new neighborhood was also a huge gift to me, as I desired to move into an emerging area so we could easily make friends with our neighbors.

Before we came to Seattle for that trip, I had a phone interview with PLCC. They offered to fly me out for a live interview and I said, "Well, I will be there next week, so it will save you the ticket." They picked me up from the hotel for the interview the day after we bought our house. While we were driving along 212th Avenue, I said, "There's our house," as it was sitting there all alone on the new street. They replied by saying, "Whoa, that's really close to the church." It turns out that it was just two miles away, a huge gift to a family who spent their life in the car in Denver.

I must mention that the search committee had been meeting for two years to fill the position to which I was hired. They had already brought in a candidate; but were turned down by him, so the committee was rather broken. They were on their knees that same December I was, asking God to do the same thing I was asking him for: to *move powerfully in their lives* and clear the path to bring the right candidate. God powerfully answered their prayers and once again went beyond by having my moving expenses covered, compliments of Bill's new employer.

After I came home from the first visit to Seattle in February, I had a heart to heart with God. I told him that I didn't know what I would be doing in Seattle, but I asked him to "fulfill the desires of my heart." I had just gotten up from the couch when the phone rang. It was Richard Oliver, the head of the search committee, telling me that they were thrilled with my minister's profile and they wanted to talk to me. Instantly I thought, "Wow, God answered my prayer within seconds!"

When it started to get serious with PLCC, I began to hear the sense of urgency in the search committee about getting someone on board quickly. I began to worry that I wouldn't have enough time to get my family settled, so I began to pray about it. One day right after I had brought this request to the Lord, I got another call from Richard Oliver telling me that they wanted me to work part time over the summer and start full time in the fall, so I would have time to get my family adjusted. Once again, God went ahead of me!

The night before I went to the first live interview with PLCC, I had a dream in which the Lord told me, *"I am calling you to these people so that you can teach, train and equip them, so they will be ready for what I want to do."* I went through the rest of the process very peacefully, knowing that it was already a done deal; God had already accomplished it.

We had planned to move in early April, but when we spoke to the high school in Sammamish, they were definite that Bonnie needed to finish chemistry in her current high school. We didn't end up moving until the beginning of June, so she could finish her sophomore year in Denver. All that time, our house continued to stay on the market, getting offers over and over; yet somehow, none of them resulted in a sale. When we finally left Denver, our house had been on the market for six months. We didn't really understand until after we moved that God had provided us with a place to live and some stability in our home, during a time of great disequilibrium; one more way that God showed his faithfulness to us in the midst of this big "move."

Our friends in Denver gave us great sendoffs; one of the best was a cleaning party in our home the night before we left. They also came to say goodbye at 6 a.m., as we left Denver for the last time. We didn't have time to let the dust settle underneath our feet when we arrived in Seattle. We moved into our beautiful new home in Sammamish on a Monday, and I began the candidating process with PLCC on Thursday. On Friday, I picked Heather up from SPU, and on Sunday, I was voted in as Pastor of Adult Ministries at PLCC. It was a whirlwind to say the least!

One of the biggest gifts to me in this move was how specific God was in showing us the way. He made it clear that he wanted us to move to Seattle by sending Heather first; I call her our Front Runner. He provided Bill with a job that challenged him and gave him much joy. He gave me peace to give up *The Journey Project*, something to which I had devoted my heart and soul. He showed us exactly where to live and answered my prayer for friendships with our neighbors. He put us right into the community where I would minister— living closer to the church than any other staff member. Finally, he answered my prayers to fulfill the desires of my heart through the ministry that I was called to lead as Pastor of Adult Ministries.

I've never had to wonder if God called me to PLCC. I can just remember all the ways that he revealed his will to me, to our family, and to the church. It truly was a miracle of God *moving* powerfully in my life: *moving* to Seattle, that is!

The Miracle of God's Word

by
Suzanne Holsten

I never did like Halloween, and even though the events of Oct. 31, 2003 had nothing to do with Halloween, the day was indeed scary and dark for my family. With my dear husband at my side, I was told that I most likely had ovarian cancer. This was confirmed within a few days, and my family and I have been fighting this disease ever since.

My dictionary defines a miracle as "an event or effect considered as a work of God." Since that diagnosis, I have experienced countless miracles. God has been and is at work in my life. Two of the miracles stand out among the many.

The first miracle is a new understanding of the power of God's word. In Hebrews 4:12, the Bible tells me that, *"The word of God is living and active. Sharper than any double-edged sword, it penetrates even to dividing soul and spirit, joints and marrow; it judges the thoughts and attitudes of the heart."* The word of God touches my whole being and not only speaks to me, but it acts on my behalf. God's word is not passive, but involved and relevant in my life today. Many times God's word lifts my spirit, corrects my wrongs, and gives me hope.

The second miracle that comes to mind is closely related, for God's word speaks of it often. That is the miracle of peace, even when the storm rages. I have felt God's peace many times, as I lay on examining tables, waiting for scans to be read, or face various surgeries. At no other time in my life have I known the reality of God's peace, like I know it now.

I am still waiting for the miracle of total healing, but I have no doubt that God is more than able to find every cancer cell and eliminate it forever. In the meantime, by God's grace, I plan to keep trusting in his living word and enjoying his promised peace.

"Rejoice in the Lord always. I will say it again: Rejoice! Let your gentleness be evident to all. The Lord is near. Do not be anxious about anything, but in everything, by prayer and petition, with thanksgiving, present your requests to God. And the peace of God, which transcends all understanding, will guard your hearts and your minds in Christ Jesus." Philippians 4:4–7

Two Words—So Little, So Much

by
Nancy Paris Howser

In 1989, my mother died at the age of eighty-nine. I flew to Illinois for her funeral and to comfort my ninety-four year old step-dad, who adored her. Sadly, he followed her into the hospital two hours after she was admitted and joined her in heaven twelve days later.

Mom's death was hard on me. She had not had an easy life. After Dad died when I was nine, it became even more difficult, as she sought to provide for the needs of a young child. In those last two years of the war, with my brothers in the service, we became very close to each other.

When I flew home after her funeral, I brought some of her things with me: her eyeglasses, some handwritten journals, a pair of gloves, photos, and other items that meant something to her and to me.

My husband Bob picked me up at the airport and after dropping me at home, left for a meeting. As darkness fell, I began pulling Mom's belongings from my suitcase in the bedroom. A deep sadness engulfed me. Tears spilled from my downcast eyes, as the full weight of her passing washed over me. With a swipe of my hand, I brushed them away, and that is the moment when I saw the message. There, spelled out on the high-low pile of the bedroom carpet where written two words. I would recognize that handwriting anywhere. The two words were written in my mother's distinctively rounded, backhand script with the funny little swept-under letter "m." They read, *my spirit.*

I blinked and looked again. Surely my eyes were playing tricks on me. But they were still there. I blinked and looked yet again. Yes, the words were still there. I stared at them and asked myself how this could be. What did they mean?

Finally, I left the room and stayed away for some minutes. When I returned, the mysterious words were gone and amazingly so was my sadness. Instead, I felt uplifted, completely exhilarated! I knew what the words meant. My mom was telling me that she was OK, that her spirit was with God.

As a Christian, I didn't doubt that there is something more after death, that we do indeed have a future. This uplifting experience reassured me of my belief and has stayed with me all these years.

Who Is God?

by
Teresa Lalk

I grew up in a Christian home. Every Sunday morning and evening, we went to church as a family. When I was fourteen years old, I gave my heart to God. I prayed and read the Bible on a regular basis and thought that my life was good and in order. Eventually I got married, and God blessed me with a loving and supportive husband, Ulrich. Then we were blessed with two healthy boys.

Ten years into our marriage, we decided to go on a family holiday to the Oregon coast for a week. We were all looking forward to a fun and relaxing time, but it turned out to be a life changing experience. God decided to turn my life around.

At 5:00 a.m., Ulrich woke me up and told me to call 911. He was out of breath and thought he was having a heart attack. My legs went numb, and I stood there motionless. I felt helpless and began to pray. I begged God not to take him away from me. I promised God that I would turn my life around and be a better Christian. That night, we ended up in the hospital. They ran all kinds of tests on Ulrich but couldn't find anything wrong. It turned out that he was having panic attacks.

Because of this experience, I started to pray more and began studying the Bible. But after awhile, I became tired of this new way of living. Soon my life went back to normal. Then, six months later, Ulrich was diagnosed with testicular cancer. The first thought that went through my mind was that God was punishing me for not changing my life. I felt so scared because I didn't know what God had planned for me.

We had just relocated to the area and were moving into our new house on a Monday. That Thursday, Ulrich went in for surgery. Afterwards he had to go for radiation treatments on a daily basis for three weeks. Some days the boys and I would go with him, and other days he would go alone. The radiation made him very tired and weak. I had to unpack the house, care for two small children and look after my husband. I quickly felt overwhelmed. I didn't know where to turn. I was too scared to turn to God and felt too embarrassed to turn to our new church. I mistakenly thought that I was strong enough to handle everything by myself. I was so used to controlling everything in my life, or at least living with the illusion that I was in control.

After Ulrich got better, I fell into a very deep depression. I felt that God was against me. I believed it was my fault that my husband got sick and that I was a terrible mother. I felt utterly worthless—that life was not worth living. I felt so alone and scared with nowhere to turn. I reached a point in my life when I felt it was not worth being a Christian. It was as if God had deserted me and there was nothing left for me. I prayed to God to take my life before I took it myself.

That Sunday, I went to church and God spoke directly to me through the words of the minister. He said that if you feel lonely and scared, or like you don't belong, you must thank God. He went on to say that when you feel like that, it is a sign that God is working in your life. He assured us that we would never completely belong on earth because our true home is in heaven. The words resonated in my heart. It was as if the sermon was meant just for me.

After that, I joined the Freedom Trek at our church. I shared my story and the pain and anger I had towards God. It was apparent that I didn't love God but feared him. I saw God as a mighty ruler that looks down on us and punishes us for being disobedient. I thought God would measure my Christianity by how long I prayed or read the Bible. If I didn't pray before bedtime, I would lie awake the whole night fearful that God would take my life. I was too scared to ask God for what I wanted in life because I believed he would give me the opposite. I was too scared to obey God because I thought he would take everything away from me, like Job in the Bible. I was afraid that obedience meant that God would take away everything that is precious to me.

It took a year of prayer, weekly meetings and guidance of a sponsor for me to realize who God really is. I learned that he is a loving God, a God who can be my friend if I will open my heart and trust in him. Up until this point, I wasn't putting God first in my life. I realized that I worshipped my husband and saw him as my Savior. I was trying to control my life and wasn't allowing God to show me the way to a better life.

Now I know that God uses the negative things in my life to teach me lessons to be a better Christian. Now I know that I won't go to hell if I am too tired to pray or read the Bible. Now I put my faith in God's promise that my future life in heaven is an inheritance that can never be taken away. Bible study is not a duty anymore. It is an exercise to become more like Jesus and draw closer to my creator.

God took the guilt, burden and fear away and gave me hope—hope for a new life with Jesus Christ, my Savior, and my best friend. This is my miracle to know that Jesus is my friend and that he will be with me forever.

The Woodpecker Chorus

by
Margaret S. (Peggy) Hendricks

A February winter day in the rainy Northwest is generally not one in which to plan an outdoor event, but February 10, 2004 was the exception. It was a warm, sunny pre-spring day. My three adult children and I stood among the tall cedar trees along a tree-lined access road.

Quietly my son read from the New Testament Book of 1 Corinthians: Chapter 15, the resurrection of Jesus Christ. Then one of my daughters carried the container of her father's ashes into the brush surrounding a particularly big cedar tree and gently scattered them. The area was near where for the past seventeen years of our fifty-three years together in marriage we had spent so happily. Silently the four of us stood in the awesome reverence of the moment.

Our silence was suddenly interrupted by the sounds of birds singing overhead. We looked up and saw a number of redheaded woodpeckers that were singing and pecking on nearby trees. The sounds and sights brought immediate smiles to our faces, as we looked at each other in amazement.

We knew it was Gods' serendipitous closing to this godly man's life, for here is the story he loved to tell about the wood-peckers: "When I was a boy in the first grade, my teacher divided the children into sections according to their singing abilities. There were the songbirds, bluebirds and robins; then there were the listening birds, and finally the woodpecker section. Yes, I was a wood-pecker!"

How could we doubt that God was smiling and winking a twinkling eye at us! Each of us felt his peace, presence and closing benediction in the sending of the woodpecker choir to welcome our loved one home.

Prepared for the Worst

by
Carra Lee Bolger

We lost our son, Joe, when he was only seventeen years old, at the end of his junior year of high school. It was quite a shock to us and everyone else who knew Joe. His passing had a huge impact on young and old alike, as he was a friend to all. Even those who didn't know Joe but read about him in the papers or heard about him on the nightly news were affected by his death. Over two thousand people came to his memorial service at Overlake Christian Church in Kirkland, Washington.

It will be ten years in May 2007, since he went home to be with the Lord. I am still hearing incredible stories of lives that are being changed and are coming to the Lord, as a direct result of having known Joe. He loved the Lord and would share his love for God with anyone who would listen. He was very involved with "Young Life" at his high school. Largely because of his direct influence, there would be over one hundred kids attending Monday night's club meeting, often at our home. The most recent time was the Monday just before his passing. He cared about his friends and their eternal destiny, and he showed it by the way he was—a very caring and fun-loving guy. He didn't have an enemy in the world.

On Saturday night, Memorial Day Weekend, 1997, Joe was boxing in a friend's backyard, with all the proper and safe gear on, to raise money for his senior class graduation party. Later we were told that after he had won all three rounds, he stepped out of the ring, bent over, then raised himself up to look at all his friends who were standing around. Then he suddenly fell to the ground. Two of his friends who were standing nearby began immediately administering CPR. A volunteer fireman who lived next door was on the scene to assist within a couple of minutes.

When the paramedics arrived, they were astounded to see how calm and controlled all the kids were. There was no evidence of drinking or drugs, and the kids were all huddled around in groups praying and crying. Our sons, John and Tommy, arrived shortly thereafter. The medics proceeded to use every extreme measure they could to revive Joe, including paddles and injections to get his heart going again. But nothing worked. The paramedic who worked on Joe could not believe that he couldn't revive him. He had never lost anyone so young before. Later he reviewed all of the tapes and recordings of the life-saving measures he had attempted, and he had done everything correctly. The next day the medics called a meeting for all the kids and parents to come to the junior high school to try to explain what had happened. They even apologized for not being able to keep Joe alive.

We arrived at the scene of Joe's death about an hour later. Friends had come to the theatre in Issaquah to escort my husband, Tom, and me to the home where Joe was. All they told us was that Joe had fallen and was being treated by the medics. It was the longest car ride of our lives! When we arrived at the home, the fire department chaplain greeted us. Tom screamed, and I felt numb. We were slowly escorted around to the back yard where we saw Joe's body draped with a white sheet. I collapsed to the ground, stone cold and shivering. I noticed that the paramedics had already left and only the police were there and a few friends.

There was some concern that Joe's boxing partner had caused his death by an injury to his head or chest. I was adamantly opposed to this accusation, and I assured them that his boxing partner did not cause Joe's death. God had simply taken him home. Later that night I was able to comfort the young man and his parents with the same words of knowledge. The reason I was so sure of what I was saying was because of something that had happened to me four months earlier.

At the end of January, I was in our bathroom when Joe came in to talk to me about something that was bothering him. He was a very conscientious boy, and he wanted to know if what he had done was terribly wrong. He had gone up to Canada with a group of friends, and they had been drinking alcohol, even though they were not of legal age. Of course, I told him that he should not have been doing that, but God would forgive him and he should not do it again. He agreed and left the room.

Just as he was leaving, I heard God say to me that Joe is like his son Jesus. I thought, how strange—no one could be that good or righteous. Then I had another realization: God was telling me that Joe would never marry. He was pure and innocent. Joe would be going home to be with God at a young age. All of these thoughts came over me like a flood. I didn't want to believe what I was thinking or hearing. I wishfully hoped that it was all just my imagination. I decided not to tell anyone, including my husband.

The divine message I received that day caused me to appreciate Joe even more and not deny his tiniest wish, even though he never asked for much anyway. I prayed that Joe would not suffer when he died. I believe God answered my prayer, because he went so quickly after the boxing match. One second he was here and the next he was in heaven with Jesus. I believe that once he got a glimpse of heaven, he knew he was home. Like our pastor said, "Why would he want to leave paradise?"

God is so good! When I was finally able to get up and walk, I kneeled down by Joe's side and pulled back the sheet from his face and touched him. Even though he was already turning cold, I prayed to God that he would bring him back to life. God's answer was an emphatic "NO!" Again, God said something that seemed very strange to me at the time, but what later made sense. He said, "He is my sacrifice." I argued, "How can that be? Jesus Christ is your sacrifice!" Now, I think I understand what God meant. So many people have turned their lives around and even come to know Jesus, not just because of Joe's influence when alive, but even more so in his death. This even impacted his own brother, Tommy, to turn his life around. He has since turned his life over to Jesus!

Two days after Joe's death I was totally convinced that God had truly spoken those words to me of truth and life, when the state's medical examiner called to give me the results of his autopsy. He told me how sorry he was to report that there was no medical cause for

Joe's death—no injury, no heart problems or stroke. I was satisfied because this confirmed everything God had said to me! I was able to call the parents of Joe's boxing partner, to give them the good news that their son had not caused Joe's death.

There were two other things the Lord told me that night that were reassuring and comforting to me. He said my family would be healed, and I would see Joe soon. The first is already coming true. My family is being healed relationally and spiritually. It has been a long and slow process, but I know that what God promises, he will fulfill.

God prepared me in a very special way for Joe's passing, but it was still terribly hard. Losing my beloved son has been the most devastating experience of my life. Nothing can fill the void he has left. But, on the other hand, I acknowledge that there has been a richness that has come into our lives as we walk our given path in the light of what God is doing and continues to do for the glory of his kingdom. He is taking us on a journey of faith that goes deeper and deeper. We are on a voyage with him that is both exciting and terrifying. All we can do is trust in God with all our heart!

DIVINE ENCOUNTERS WITH GOD

As they approached the village to which they were going, Jesus acted as if he were going farther. But they urged him strongly, "Stay with us, for it is nearly evening; the day is almost over." So he went in to stay with them. When he was at the table with them, he took bread, gave thanks, broke it and began to give it to them. Then their eyes were opened and they recognized him, and he disappeared from their sight. They asked each other, "Were not our hearts burning within us while he talked with us on the road and opened the Scriptures to us?" They got up and returned at once to Jerusalem. There they found the Eleven and those with them, assembled together saying, "It is true! The Lord has risen and has appeared to Simon." Then the two told what had happened on the way, and how Jesus was recognized by them when he broke bread.

Luke 24: 28–35

Accident in the Dakotas

by
Linda Knodel

On the morning of July 8, 2005, my husband Ron and I left Hurdsfield, North Dakota to drive home after attending his high school reunion. We planned to stop in Medora on our way back to see a much spoken about musical.

As we headed west on Interstate 94, we passed the first exit to Medora. I told Ron that we just missed our exit. He stated, "No, I think there is another one further up the road." Within two minutes, we could see in the distance a woman in the middle of the highway frantically waving her arms. Immediately we slowed down. As we drew nearer, we were gripped by the grim fact that we had just come upon an accident. We quickly pulled our truck over to the shoulder and ran to the scene to offer our help. Little did we know that this woman was the mother of one of the accident victims.

For the next hour, what followed was a surreal scene—one that I had never before been a part of in my life. It was a very scorching one hundred degrees, and the air pressed down on us like a suffocating blanket. The Badlands were looming over my shoulder from every angle; they were white, crusty, and unforgiving. The heat was rising from the asphalt in waves that left me feeling like I would stick to the road if I stopped and stood in one place for any length of time.

When we ran from our truck, I saw a young man lying on the road. He was quiet and still. He appeared to be unconscious and was not in any visible pain. Every step I took toward him, I felt like bricks were holding down my feet. I was scared and breathless and confused because as a registered nurse, I was sure I should know just how to handle this scene. A woman ran up behind me, she sat on the ground next to him and turned him over in her lap. She kept repeating, "He has a pulse, and I think he is breathing."

I heard the woman who had waved us down frantically trying to talk to someone at 911 on her cell phone. My husband took the phone from her, was able to make a calm connection to the dispatcher, and was told that help was on the way. He then handed me the phone so that I could stay with the dispatcher to give additional details. The closest town of any size was Dickenson, which was nearly thirty miles away. I knew that was where the help would come from and it would take time. Each precious minute would seem like an hour in a dire situation as this was.

During those frightful minutes, I realized there was a baby boy still inside the car and another child, a little girl about ten or eleven years old, down the ditch in the tall grass. Ron rushed to her side and stayed with her the entire time. Others who had now reached the scene were able to release the baby boy from the vehicle with the help of the woman who had originally flagged us down. Another woman took him to a shaded spot near a van, held him there and soothed him. As I found out later, this baby boy was the son of the young man lying in the road and the grandson of the woman who freed him from the van.

I then found my way back to the young woman sitting by the side of the road. Another woman was with her speaking very softly and lovingly to her. She looked at me and asked where her husband was. I knew that he had to be the young man who was lying on the road behind her. I told her that he was with some very kind folks who were attending to him. This was true, as a very kind woman had gone to care for the young man. She took his pulse and tried as best she could to keep him stable.

A strange silence hung over the scene, a silence that seemed deafening to me. But through it all, I felt the absolute presence of Our Lord and Savior, Jesus Christ amidst the tragedy. It brought a comforting peace to me in the middle of a frantic situation. When we first arrived on the scene, my first reaction was to call out, "Lord, are you here?" I felt compelled to say this repeatedly.

When I went to the young woman's side, I asked her if she knew that Jesus was present and taking care of the situation. I asked her if we could pray right then and there. I believe she knew that God and his angels were close by. The mountains facing us appeared harsh and unforgiving, yet our prayers seemed to ascend to Heaven on the heat waves rising from the asphalt that day.

At one point while sitting with this young woman, I turned around to see the young man, her husband, lying on the road. In that moment, my heart had an amazing vision. I saw Jesus Christ beside him, lovingly cradling him in his arms. He was comforting him and freeing him from his human body. It was as if Jesus was saying to him, "It is your time to go now. Peace be with you."

After all of the emergency vehicles had arrived and everyone was transported to the hospital, we were able to leave the scene of the accident. That night we stayed in a motel in Medora. We were both reeling from the day's horrific events and were only able to reflect that our faith is what had kept us going through this tragic event.

That evening I called Dickinson Hospital, hoping to learn of the fate of the passengers. I knew in my heart that due to privacy issues, they would not release any information to me, but I could not help but wonder and pray for some answers.

The next morning we awoke early and got a local newspaper, which gave the names and minimal information related to the accident. I saved the paper, and when we returned home, I went online to see if I could find out any other details. I found out that thankfully the young woman and two children had survived, but sadly, the young man had died at the scene of the accident. His name was Kelly.

Following this harrowing experience, I was filled with grief and pain for the family of the young man. Since that fateful day when Ron and I missed our exit and came upon the accident, I have gone over the events thousands of times in my mind. I took my grief to our Pastor and the grief ministry team at church for solace.

Contacting the young man's family through a letter, which told them that he was completely at peace and in the presence of our Lord when he died, has helped in my healing process. Three days after I mailed the letter, I received a phone call on my answering machine. A tiny voice said, "This is Kristin. I was the girl sitting by the road. We have your letter. Please call this hospital in Bismarck, North Dakota.

I was shaking fiercely as I dialed the number. When the receptionist answered, she said they had no one by that name there. At that point, I was frantic. I kept explaining to her that I had a message from that number and would she please find Kristin. She insisted that there was no one by that name listed in the hospital. Finally, out of frustration, I pleaded with her to connect me with the pediatric unit taking a chance that just maybe the baby was the patient and she was there with him. When the phone was answered, I blurted out my confusion about the call and conveyed to the woman who answered that I was weary with worry that I would not find her.

She stopped me mid sentence and said, "Are you the woman that wrote the letter?" I was dumbfounded. Within seconds, Kristin came on the line. I spoke to her and she said, "I recognize your voice as the one who prayed by the side of the road with me." She said that the letter I sent to Kelly's parents went from their home in Dickinson to Bismarck where the rest of the family had congregated at the hospital where Kristin and her sister, the ten year old girl were patients. As it turns out, they desperately needed my letter to begin to grasp what happened that day on a hot stretch of highway that turned their ride to a family picnic outing into the loss of a beloved son, husband and father.

From that day forward we were bonded. We called each other frequently to get updates on the family's recovery. Kristin suffered multiple fractures to her pelvis and sustained disc problems as well as a laceration on her back that required one hundred stitches. Her sister Taylor, who was thrown from the car into the ditch, was in very serious condition, as she suffered brain trauma. Thankfully Kristin, her sister Taylor and the baby Dietric, all survived the accident.

In the year since the accident, by the grace of our Lord and Savior Jesus Christ, they have been healed from their physical wounds. With the help of many who love them, are mending their hearts as well. Looking back on this tragic event, I believe that God had a hand in Ron and me missing our turn and being at the scene of the accident that day. For in God's master plan, truly there are no accidents in life.

The Business of Fulfillment

by
Jay Nyce

Throughout my career, I've had many different jobs and positions, but in my heart, I felt that I should be running my own business. Most of the time, I found my jobs to be frustrating, unfulfilling and confining. So often I found that I had to compromise my values in order to work for someone else, which created conflicts in the workplace. Over time, I discovered that my motives for working had changed dramatically. Early in my career, being in business was primarily to bring home a paycheck and for other personal gain, but eventually I made a one hundred and eighty degree shift. I came to believe that a company should be run with Biblical principals at the heart of the business model, treating employees, customers and suppliers with respect. I had come to a critical point in my career. I now desired a position where I could be more true to my character and values and could expand God's kingdom in the workplace.

During this time, I was reading the Bible, praying and journaling consistently. Day after day I poured my heart out to God letting him know the desires for my career to take a new direction—one in which I could be in charge. On the morning of May 10, 2002 in my home office, I prayerfully told God my desire to lead a business for him. Later when I was riding my exercise bike, I experienced a remarkable phenomenon. Suddenly, Jesus came down through the ceiling, sat in my desk chair, and spoke to me. Immediately I stopped pedaling and stared at the amazing sight in front of me. He spoke these exact words to me, "I know you've been praying about your calling. I'm going to get you that business." It was the most vivid image of Jesus that I have ever seen. Then he was gone.

Soon afterwards, I went downstairs and met my wife Tina. I said, "You won't believe what just happened!" Then I told her the dramatic experience in detail. The first thing she said was, "What was he wearing?" I told her that he looked like the Jesus from pictures we normally see at church or in books. He had long hair and a beard, and wore a tunic and sandals laced up to just below his knees.

From that point on, I released my control of trying to get a business on my own. I was filled with a sense of peace that Jesus was going to supply me with my calling in my career and the longing of my heart would one day be fulfilled. Soon after my miraculous encounter with Jesus, things started falling into place for me business-wise.

Later that year I was meditating on Proverbs 13:12 *"...but a longing fulfilled is a tree of life"* and Proverbs 13:19 *"A longing fulfilled is sweet to the soul..."* In my journal that day, I asked myself what my longing was and wrote these words: "Some close friends, a family business, and a happy, peaceful and joyful daughter." There it was again—my desire to have my own business. I didn't want to push the idea on Tina, so I continued to wait for God's promise to be fulfilled.

Then in the summer of 2005, out of the blue, Tina asked if I would join her business, Nyce Gardens, and expand it from a design company only to a design and installation business. I gladly accepted her offer and we began working together on the endeavor. Recently Nyce Gardens has been able to expand God's kingdom by leading the landscape design and installation team for PLCC's Mission in Targu Jiu, Romania. It was an incredible experience for our family.

Since we've been working together expanding our family business, I finally feel fulfilled in my career. I am not surprised that Jesus continues to come through on his promises for my life. I am often reminded of a Bible passage from 1 Thessalonians 4:11–12 that has significant meaning to me: *"Make it your ambition to lead a quiet life, to mind your own business and to work with your hands, just as we told you, so that your daily life may win the respect of outsiders and so that you will not be dependant on anybody."*

A True Friend In Jesus

by
Susan R. Schlepp

D eath hadn't significantly impacted my life, until I was nineteen years old. My sophomore year of college had just
wrapped up, and I had recently begun working as a summer
intern at my brother's international marketing company.

When I headed off to college after high school, I drifted away
from church, only attending services on the major holidays when I
visited my family. This was a time in my life when I was beginning
to get comfortable in my own skin and tentatively trying newfound
independence on for size.

Several months before, my sister's best friend had moved to the
area to start working for my brother as an Account Executive. Her
career was taking off, and her future with the company looked
promising. When I arrived on the scene, we hit it off right away. I
looked up to her almost instantly. She had a dynamic personality cou-
pled with a spontaneity and love of life that was contagious. It
seemed to me like she could hold her own with anyone, in any situation. At twenty-six, she was certainly worldlier than any of my other
friends.

For a couple of precious weeks we chummed around together. I
had found a new friend and mentor, and was anxious to suck up every
drop of our time together. I was thrilled to go nightclubbing with her
one evening. Driving home that night, the summer stretched out

ahead of me like a sweet promise of more fun times to come.

The next morning I honked repeatedly outside of the apartment she had recently moved into, as I was late for work. The night before, she had asked me to pick her up because her sports coup convertible was in the shop. She even drove a cool car. When she didn't appear, I went to her door to knock, only to find a scrawled note taped to it stating that she couldn't make it to work and would call me later. Now running really late, I crumpled up the note and tossed it in my purse failing to notice that it was signed with her first initial and last name.

As the day wore on and she was still a no show at work, my stomach began to tighten like a vice. The whole thing wasn't sitting right with me. Throughout the day, I called and recalled her phone number, letting it ring and ring. There was no answer. I dug the crinkled note out of my purse, read, and reread it. The signature seemed odd. As my fears deepened, the vice tightened. I began to discern that something was terribly wrong.

After work, I met my brother at his home. He was angry with her for missing an important client presentation. I expressed my fears that something terrible might have happened to her. He instructed me to drive to her apartment and see if I could get in. He thought she might have left a note or would show up while I was there. I absolutely did not want to go over to her apartment alone and begged him to come with me.

"What if she's dead?" I pleaded.

He assured me everything would be fine and persuaded me to go by myself.

As I began the ten-minute drive to her apartment, the vice in my stomach completely clamped shut. Every bell and whistle that my gut instincts had at their disposal began going off simultaneously, as I headed down a long, straight stretch of road. I recall my knuckles turning white from my death grip on the steering wheel. Soon I was in a full-blown panic. This was not an emotional state I was familiar with, which made it even more terrifying. Except for the occasional bump in the road, my life had largely been over smooth terrain. That was all about to change.

At the pinnacle of my terror, suddenly a brilliant light descended through the roof of the car. Unconditional love and peace swept through my body from head to toe. Instantly my panic and fear were replaced with calm and control. I felt a familiar presence in the car with me, someone who knew me completely, and someone who I knew in return, even though I had never met him before. There was absolutely no doubt who it was. In the most critical moment of my entire life, Jesus Christ himself was there to guide me through it.

For the next minute or two, in what I can only describe as mental telepathy, he warned and prepared me for what I was about to encounter. From that moment on, I was on autopilot.

Arriving at my friend's apartment, I asked a security guard to let me inside with a master key from the office. I found out later that he was only eighteen years old and had been on the job just a few days. Neither of us noticed that the jalousie window on the kitchen door was broken and that the inner screen had been sliced with a knife.

As we entered the kitchen, I noticed several knives lined up like soldiers on the short kitchen counter, as if resting from some recent duty they had performed. Stepping into the living room, I saw that all of the window shades were tightly shut. My eyes struggled to adjust to the abrupt change from direct sunlight to the eerie darkness inside.

While the security guard searched the living room, I turned to the bedroom on my left. The door was open, and I immediately noticed an oscillating fan on the floor. It was blowing towards the bed that was just out of sight from where I stood. Tentatively I took one step into the room and looked toward the bed. My friend was lying motionless with the covers pulled up to her chin. Her face was covered with an oily film that gave her fair skin an unnatural tone. Her beautiful, raven black hair was slicked back, and her eyes were wide-open. When I looked into them, I saw that while it was my friend's body, mercifully my friend wasn't there any longer. Staring back at me was death with absolute finality.

Heeding Jesus Christ's earlier warning, I knew not to go any closer. I backed out of the room and unwilling to accept what I knew to be true, I shakily asked the security guard to check on her. How much I wish I could take back that request and spare him the horror of what he witnessed, when he pulled back the covers. He discovered my friend's mutilated body.

Rushing into the living room he screamed, "We have to get out of here now!"

Together we ran to the apartment office and called the police. Then I called my brother and told him the horrific news. Our friend had been brutally murdered. As the parade of emergency vehicles arrived, still on autopilot, I sat on the curb and quietly waited for all that was to follow.

That night at a downtown police station, I was questioned at length to find out if I had any information that would help find her killer. I gave the detectives the crumpled note from her door that was still in my purse. It would soon become a key piece of evidence in the manhunt that was underway.

Later I learned that sometime before she was killed in the middle of the night, my friend told the murderer that someone would be picking her up for work that morning, probably hoping that he would leave. The murderer had written the note I retrieved from her door, taking her first initial and last name from her mailbox for the signature. The note was the means for him to gain more time in her apartment throughout the next day.

Looking back, my friend may have saved my life. I dread the thought of what might have happened if she hadn't told him that I would be picking her up. I might have come face to face with the murderer, instead of a note. It was also chilling to think that we had discussed my moving in with her only a short time before. I could easily have been there that night.

Thankfully, the murderer was caught quickly afterwards. He was taken into custody and after lengthy questioning, confessed to the heinous crimes of breaking into her apartment, brutally murdering her and trying to cover up the evidence by inflicting further unspeakable acts of violence to her.

After being apprehended, the murderer was linked to other violent crimes in the area. When the state brought formal charges against him, he waived his rights to a trial in order to avoid the death penalty. My friend's family and the other victims, including myself, gave testimony to the judge about the horrible impact his crimes had on our lives. I was struck by what a miracle it was that the others had survived his separate and viscous attacks. His malicious crimes had taken so much from so many, and the full impact had not yet been felt.

Currently he is serving consecutive life sentences in a maximum-security penitentiary and unbelievably may be eligible for parole in the future. I try to have faith that our system will see that a life sentence is truly a life sentence in his case. God has since prepared me for a day when I may need to appear in front of a parole board to stand up for justice to keep her killer behind bars.

Almost two decades have passed since my friend's death and the divine intervention from Jesus Christ that warned and protected me from witnessing the worst of it. He prepared me for the grizzly murder scene I was about to witness. Certainly with the foreknowledge, I was spared the gruesome sight of her body. Even when my sister chastised me for not rushing to our friend's side when I saw her lying there, I was reluctant to share my interaction with Christ. My natural instinct was to rush to her, but Jesus had warned me not to and I had obeyed. He also supernaturally provided me with the strength and calm to get through that horrible night and all that was to follow. I am forever thankful for his divine intervention.

This harsh experience caused a loss of innocence that profoundly changed me from that point forward. I witnessed firsthand how far reaching a single act of evil can extend. Most importantly, I experienced merciful intervention from a loving God who truly cares about the trials that each of us face. I pondered whether God had work for me to do later in life, and he knew that my sensitive soul might not have completely recovered from such a sight.

I have to admit that for a time, I was angry with God too. Why did I have to be the one to find her? I thought others would see me differently from then on, or if they ever found out about it in the future. It seemed like an ugly, permanent blight on my life. Over the past twenty plus years, I have come to realize that sharing this experience, as hard as it is, can draw others nearer to God. My experience is a testimony to the love of God.

My family and I will forever be linked to my friend's family through shared grief and the resulting celebration of her life. Recently, her mother told me that over the years since the murder, during their lowest times, she and her husband have felt their daughter's presence and witnessed signs they feel certain were sent by her to comfort them.

One such time was when her father was walking alone in their backyard shortly after her death, overcome with grief and a flood of conflicting emotions about her murder. Suddenly a loving force swept over him and his daughter's voice said, "I'm OK Dad. Go on with your life. Please don't hate."

Her mother also told me that as hard as it is to live with their loss, amazingly, good things have come from tragedy. After their daughter's murder, they became active in a national organization that defends victim's rights. They have impacted and been touched by many people who they would not have known otherwise, proving that God truly brings forth goodness out of despicable acts of evil.

My sister shared with me that our friend told her on more than one occasion that somehow she knew she was going to die young and in a tragic way. We both wonder if this was God's way of preparing her for her fate on earth. I choose to believe that she did not suffer, but was delivered from the ordeal into the loving hands of her creator. I feel so privileged to have known her and sometimes sense her smiling down on me from a better place.

A few days before she died, my girlfriend heard my fears and anxieties about the future and said these simple words, "Susan, you should go for it more in life." Her encouragement has stayed with me over the years, as has the divine intervention that protected me that fateful day.

Seeing Jesus

by
Helen Boyer

The year 2006 has been the most explosive period of spiritual growth that I have ever experienced. A center of this transformation for me has been the Healing Prayer Trek group I am so fortunate to have found, led by Pastor Tamara at PLCC. The class has joined prayer and scripture for me in a way that led me to become more aware of the constant presence of God everywhere and in the ways that prayer can release God's power through the Holy Spirit in us.

In my daily prayer practice, I use stretching and movement to attune myself to the Lord, as a vestibule through which I enter into a quiet space of contemplation, a place Jesus spoke of in "The Sermon on the Mount" in Matthew 6:6: *"When you pray, go into your room, close the door and pray to your Father, who is unseen..."* One day as I was moving through my opening sequence, I passed through that vestibule and became aware of Jesus moving together with me, mirroring me, or was I mirroring him? It was as if we were dancing together. He was smiling at me, and I had a sensation of warmth, comfort, joy and communion. It was pure bliss.

Another time, the prayer trek team was assembled in the sanctuary at the beginning of our first healing prayer service. Cora Lombardi was leading us in an opening prayer. Without actually seeing him, I became aware of Jesus at the altar. I felt his calm, joyful, deliberate presence, directing and arranging things. Then at one point, he swept his arm toward me. At first, I saw just his hand, and a loose white sleeve against his arm. I watched him gesture toward me with a gentle lifted finger, like God reaching toward Adam in Michelangelo's painting on the ceiling of the Sistine Chapel. I felt something like a mild electric shock that went through my body from head to toe and to the tips of my fingers. It was a healing, a balm, a greeting, recognition, an acknowledgement, an anointing, and a reinforcement of the divine presence of the Holy Spirit in me. It took my breath away. As I raised my eyes, Jesus came fully into view, clothed in a white robe. I watched as he gestured toward others, seen and unseen. It was a moment out of the flow of time as I know it.

Later, I was encouraged to share this experience when Pastor Tamara told the prayer team that she had seen Jesus' outline in white at the altar table lifting his hands towards us. I have been so blessed this year by a heightened awareness of God through prayer. I am learning, as Mother Teresa taught, that I can see Jesus everywhere, in every person, if I look with my heart, and that gives me joy all day long.

Deliverance

by
Elizabeth Ashley Zorich

In January 2004, I began the New Year with the realization that I had reached rock bottom. Everything in my life was falling apart: my health, my marriage, my family, and my finances. In the fall of 2003, I had been diagnosed with Multiple Sclerosis (MS), which came on suddenly. My diagnosis was confirmed by MRI scans at a Neurology Office in Kirkland, WA which seemed to seal my fate. The disease progressed quickly through my body, particularly on my left side. I lost most of the use of my left leg, and both of my arms were getting weaker by the day. My eyesight was also becoming blurry. I was terrified by the doctor's treatment recommendations, but sensed that God would guide me to the right remedy.

To make matters worse, by Christmas of 2003, shortly after being diagnosed with MS, my husband abruptly told me he wanted a divorce. At the same time, every member of my extended family was involved in one kind of turmoil or another. No one was getting along or even talking to each other. Still worse, my financial resources were limited.

It seemed that I was facing all of these crises alone, but amazingly, God surrounded me with Christians who helped me to work through each struggle that I was wrestling with. It was at this point—the very lowest point of my life that I knew I was ready to become a Christian and turn my life over to Jesus. I had been attending a weekly Bible Study with a wonderful group of women on the Plateau in Sammamish, WA. I shared with them the struggles that I faced, and on two occasions, they placed their hands on me and prayed that Jesus would change my life.

On January 27, 2004 while meeting in my home with the Stephen's Minister that PLCC had set me up with, I became a Christian by repenting of my sins and accepting Jesus Christ into my life as my Lord and Savior. When we were finished praying, she looked at me, smiled and said, "Now your life will never be the same." At the time, I didn't have a clue what she meant. I hadn't grown up in a religious home, other than being baptized as an infant, so I didn't know Jesus or what it truly meant to be a Christian. But I did feel a remarkable sense of joy and expectation having made the leap of faith.

That night when I went to sleep, I said a prayer thanking God for bringing the Stephen's Minister and the other Christian women into my life. Then I drifted off to sleep. The next thing I knew I was looking up at Jesus. He was floating in the air a few feet above a grassy hill. On the hill to his left, he had his hand resting on the bow of an old style, wooden fishing boat. At the far end of boat, a few people were getting seated, as if they were preparing for a trip. They seemed happy and peaceful as they prepared to depart. I couldn't help but notice that Jesus' clothing was made of sparkling white light.

He didn't say a word at first. Then in the sky above us, louder than thunder, I heard our heavenly Father's voice boom, "DELIVERANCE!" I was awestruck. I knew the message was meant for me. I looked at Jesus again and he looked at me.

Then he asked, "Do you see my boat here?"

I said, "Yes."

He replied, "Do you see that there are not very many people in it yet?"

Again, I said, "Yes."

Then Jesus asked me, "Will you help me bring more people to my boat?"

I replied a resounding, "Yes!"

I found that I was smiling at him and he was smiling back at me. When all of this was happening to me, I knew that I wasn't dreaming. Somehow, some way, I was actually there with Jesus. I could feel the soft ground under my feet and smell the sweet air. It was unlike any dream I had ever had. The first thing I said to myself when I opened my eyes was, "I was just with Jesus!"

From that point on I was a new person. All of a sudden, dramatic changes began to happen to me. I found that now I couldn't stand to hear anyone take the Lord's name in vain, which had been a common occurrence in my childhood. I wanted to eat healthier and found myself suddenly attracted to Christian music. I started to go to church, read the Bible and pray more than I ever had before. Jesus was always on my mind. I knew that I loved him. He was there for me unlike any person had ever been in my life. I began to rely on him for everything. I was still so frightened by the progression of the MS throughout my body that one day I laid face down on the floor of my home. In that quiet moment between my creator and myself, I laid down my life to Jesus. No matter what the outcome, I submitted my life to him completely.

Although I was still struggling with MS, gradually day by day my life became better and better. In February 2004, God led me back to that same group of women from the Plateau. During the Bible Study, I shared with them the remarkable vision I had of Jesus with the boat. They gathered around me, placed their hands on me including my legs and began to fervently pray. At one point, they shouted out, "Lord, you've asked Elizabeth to bring people to your boat. Lord, she needs her legs to go out into the world and do this for you!" I had never been prayed over like this before. The old Elizabeth would have thought it was kind of bizarre. I had always thought that Christians seemed too happy, and I didn't know why. The new Elizabeth now knew the reason why. They had Jesus in their lives, and now I did too! The experience of being prayed for that day was both beautiful and real.

I thought the dramatic dream I had of Jesus and the boat was powerful enough; I wasn't prepared for what would happen next. This experience shook me to the core of my being. On May 24, 2004 between 9 and 10 p.m., I was sitting on my bed alone with my black lab, Gypsy. I opened up my Bible and began flipping through it to find a scripture to read before bed. Straight ahead of me was a window with the shade pulled up. It was completely dark out and the only reflection in the glass came from the lamp that was on the nightstand beside me. As I started to pray for comfort and strength, something started to happen to me. My heart started racing, and a strange sensation began to come over me. It felt like there was a highly charged energy in the room. I knew something really big was about to happen. Immediately, I sat up trying to figure out if I was experiencing a medical problem that I needed to get help for. I was in a panic. I stood up, grabbed the phone and then hung it up again. I literally thought I was going to heaven. Out of fear of the unknown, I found myself saying, "No, no, no, no, no!"

Then I sat down on the bed in silence trying to get a grip on myself, when suddenly a euphoric sedated feeling came over my body. I could see and hear perfectly, but I couldn't move very well. I felt so weak and heavy, but it wasn't a scary feeling. It was very calming and warm. Right then Jesus appeared in my room on the glass of the window looking right at me. Immediately an inner dialog began, and I was told, "Do not fear. I am your Savior Jesus Christ. You are not dying. Calm down." I kept thinking, "I'm dying! I'm dying!" He kept repeating, "Calm down child. You are not dying. It is not your time." Soon, I realized that I was fine and that it was really Jesus. My mind became calm, and I was able to listen to him.

Over the next hour, Jesus filled me with information. He told me that "Heavenly Father" had been preparing me for this moment for my entire life. He reminded me how often in my childhood I had felt different from everyone else, how I never seemed to fit in. He told me that I had spiritual gifts that would be increased upon by God to fulfill my true mission on earth including: prophesy, spirit discernment, and healing, among others. He told me that he knew I was strong enough to be a soldier for God. He confirmed some things for me and even let me ask some questions. During this time, he showed me things from my past, present and glimpses of how I would be using these gifts to help others in the future. Jesus said, "Do not worry about who or when or how. Those dates and times are not for you to know right now." At one point, I found myself on the floor bowing in front of Jesus with tears streaming down my face, and I didn't know how I had gotten there. One thing I knew for sure, I didn't want to be out of his presence—ever. Then I found myself back on the bed again.

My dog, Gypsy, jumped down off the bed with her tail wagging happily and went to the window. She leaped up with her paws on the windowsill and licked the glass where Jesus' face was. Then she jumped down and turned her head quickly in three different directions at the same time that I did, as three angels appeared above us:

to the right, left and behind me. They looked like glistening white light. Jesus told me that the angels were there to do some healing work over my body. He said I would have renewed strength as a result. The three angels came toward me and enveloped me into the light that radiated heavenly healing through my body.

The incredible experience lasted a couple of minutes. Then Jesus finished the conversation with me, and I felt him beginning to pull away. He reassured me that he would talk with me again soon. In my mind, I immediately said, "Don't leave me. I don't want you to go." He replied, "Do not fear. I am always with you. I will now bring your physical body back to feeling reality again, but my image will remain here in your room until you go to sleep." It did.

August 17, 2004 Jesus kept his promise to meet with me again. Early that evening I was upstairs sitting on the floor looking through a box of books. I opened up a large, colorful Easter book and began flipping through it. When I got to the page that showed a beautiful illustration of the resurrection of Jesus, the euphoric, weak sensation that I had felt before started again. This time, I was more prepared for what was about to unfold. As I stared at the picture of Jesus, I grew physically weaker. The weaker I became, the brighter the picture grew. The vivid colors became actual light radiating around him. Then the inner dialog with Christ began. Again, he assured me by saying, "Do not fear child. I am your Savior Jesus Christ. You will be working in a healing ministry very soon helping very ill people. Do not worry about who or when or how. Those dates and times are not for you to know right now." As Jesus was speaking, the same glowing light that was radiating from the picture of him in the book was now spinning around my hands. It was the most brilliant display of multi-colors I had ever seen, like an amazing rainbow that was spinning so fast that my hands became warm from the phenomenon. As I was witnessing it, Jesus said, "I have bestowed upon your hands the gift of healing." By December that year, God led me to a healing ministry in Issaquah, WA working closely with a pastor, just as Jesus said.

January 4, 2005 I was praying in my bedroom and the now familiar euphoric, heavy sensation came over me. This time it seemed a little lighter to me, or maybe it was just that I was getting used to it. I saw the same white light, as when the three angels had appeared, radiating in front of me. Then the inner dialog with Jesus began. He said he was about to anoint my eyes to increase the spiritual sight that I already had. He told me not to fear, as I would see more of what I am already able to see and things that I have never seen before. He cautioned me that I would now see the enemy easier than I had previously. Again, he told me not to fear. He then said, "Do not be afraid. The angels are going to come close to your face. From left to right your vision will become cloudy for two to three seconds." He said that for the next two weeks, I would have headaches and some shooting pains and my eyes would go cloudy, then they would be fine.

Since then, everything Jesus said to me has come to pass. I started working at the healing ministry on a more regular basis with some critically ill clients and others with major illnesses. The Lord quickly showed me that my newly anointed hands and eyes worked together to bring healing to the people who came to us for help. The pastor and I saw two to three clients per week for six to twelve months at a time. The Lord was miraculously making them well through us. One of our clients was a fifty-two year old man with a rare, aggressive pancreatic cancer who had been told by his doctors that he had a short time to live. Another was a professor whose eyesight had been severely impaired by strokes behind his eyes. His doctors told him that blindness was imminent. Over that period with our weekly prayers and healing work, both clients became completely well and returned to work.

During this time, I was dealing with still more personal tragedy and stress, but Jesus kept me strong and well throughout. He continues to meet with me and guide me on my spiritual journey. One of the more recent times he visited me, he reminded me that the Multiple Sclerosis does still linger in my body, but he keeps it at bay so I can stay well and strong to fulfill my mission on earth. He told me that we must submit every worry and care to him. He assured me that he is always with us whether we know it or not. I for one know it to be true and put my trust in him completely.

After being made well by Jesus, I promised to go forward and continue his ministry as long as he allows me to. My life is completely in his hands. My body is a vessel for the Holy Spirit to do God's work. I would never, ever, want to go back to living blindly, not knowing that my Savior was right there all along. The dark veil has been miraculously lifted from my eyes, and I am no longer blind.

Once I accepted Jesus Christ as my Lord and Savior, my eyes were open to the truth, and just as the Stephen's Minister had promised— my life would never be the same.

Straight to the Heart

by
Jay Nyce

One spring, my wife Tina and I traveled to North Carolina to attend her niece's wedding. Tina's brother Brent is a founding pastor of a Sovereign Grace Church in Charlotte. We were excited to experience worship there. After the wedding, we went to the worship service on Sunday morning. During one of the songs of praise, I glanced up at the ceiling and saw an image of Jesus hovering in the air. I watched as it began whirling faster and faster like a cyclone. Suddenly it dropped down and went straight into my heart. The sensation startled me and momentarily took my breath away. It felt like the Holy Spirit had instantly filled me. It was an amazing spiritual experience.

God is Love

by
Charlotte Morin

W hen I was pregnant with my second son, there were some early medical red flags, but as the pregnancy progressed, it seemed that all indicators were positive. So when it came time for me to have the usual mid-term screening tests, I wasn't too concerned. Sadly, a few days after the tests, my husband and I got a call from the geneticist who told us that there was a fifty percent chance that this child had Down's syndrome. She went on to explain that even if it wasn't Down's syndrome, the kind of test results we got back usually meant that something was very seriously wrong with the baby.

Of course, we were stunned by this news. We spent many hours pondering what we should do, what the future would hold if this child lived, and so on. One night I was particularly sad. I was facing up to the reality that if this child were born severely handicapped, it would undoubtedly have far-reaching consequences for our family—consequences that could potentially last the rest of our lives. We knew people who had been in a similar situation, which made it easy to envision in explicit detail the enormous amounts of emotion, time, and money that would be required with potentially little effect.

I cried for a long time that night, and then there came a time when I was just too tired and too numb to shed any more tears. At that point, I went to the kitchen for a piece of toast.

For several years before this happened, I had become quite

ambivalent about God and even angry with him. I certainly wasn't expecting to encounter God that night, although I was attempting, as best I could, to accept what was happening to me and reach out to him for help.

It is difficult to find adequate words to describe what happened next. All I know is that I was standing there by the toaster, and then suddenly, I wasn't. I was in the presence of God. People I have shared this experience with have asked me what I saw and heard in that moment. Honestly, I didn't see or hear anything. The best I can say is that God bypassed those senses and dealt directly with my heart and soul.

Immediately I had two impressions. First, God is…far bigger than I could have ever imagined. I had the sense of being an ant, or something microscopic, standing at the foot of the largest mountain in the universe. Compared to that mountain, my moments of sorrow, indeed my whole life seemed utterly insignificant to me. It reminds me of when Mount St. Helens was threatening to erupt in 1980. I recall hearing about a few people who refused to be evacuated because they really didn't believe that the eruption would be very dangerous. In reality, the power of the explosion erased them in seconds. Standing at the foot of that mountain, any preconceived ideas I had of somehow negotiating with God died instantly.

This experience should have been terrifying. Strangely, it wasn't because of the second thing that happened. I experienced that God is…love. From the moment I was in his presence, I was completely enveloped, bathed, and almost drowning in the most intense love imaginable. I had heard it said, "God is love." Now I knew it was true. Even though I understood that in one sense I was nothing in front of that enormous presence, God himself knew my name and everything about me. He understood my life and my sorrow completely.

I can't say for sure how long I was "gone." But when the journey was over and I returned to the kitchen, I knew deep in my heart that whatever happened in my future, I would be, in the most profound sense, "safe."

God never promised me that my pregnancy would have a happy ending. Several weeks later, in fact, we buried the tiny body of our son, Christopher. On his tombstone, we put his name, date, and the words, "Safe in Heaven." He is indeed safe there, as he could never have been here on earth. Someday we will join him on the mountain and live there forever.

The Parable of the Shells

by
Susan R. Schlepp

It was a crisp Saturday morning on March 4, 2000 when I set out alone on a walk that would forever change my life. Any day in the Pacific Northwest not involving rain is a blessed event in my book. This particular day would prove to be blessed in a much bigger way.

My husband had generously agreed to take full charge of our five-month-old daughter for the weekend, allowing me to attend a Writer's Conference with a girlfriend on an island near Seattle. I was hoping to find a publisher for some children's books that I had written and was anxious to attend a workshop on writing for the children's marketplace. I was also yearning to have some time to clear my head.

Having left the corporate grind a few years prior to pursue more creative endeavors, I was anxious to achieve some tangible success with the fruits from those labors. I was used to pulling my weight around the house financially and not contributing to our bottom line was tough for me to take. I had a hard time equating the work I did as a homemaker, as having any real value in the grand scheme of things. Up until that point, I had come up empty with my writing, only managing to get a few short stories and some poems published and not for a dollar figure worth writing home about. I had also come very close to selling a screenplay, but that hadn't panned out either.

Motherhood hadn't yet lived up to my expectations, and I had become disenchanted with just about everything else in my life too. My pregnancy had been difficult, and I was totally unprepared for the excruciating pain of childbirth. They don't call it labor for nothing! To make matters worse, immediately after delivering our daughter, I was zapped with postpartum anxiety and depression that stubbornly refused to release its grasp on me, no matter what I tried. It was taking a real toll on my life.

I just wanted to feel like my old self again and enjoy our little girl, the daughter we so wanted, anticipated and loved. Hormonally I was out of whack, and although I was functioning, I refused to accept that this was as good as I could feel. I was growing impatient with the doctors we consulted and their inability to help me. I desperately needed to get my arms around the worries I was wrestling with. This weekend was my chance to do that.

Awakening early, I set off for a walk on a long stretch of beach a couple blocks from the house where my friend and I were staying. That night had been a restless one, as I grappled with my inability to make things right in my life. Stepping onto the sand, I noticed that the tide was out and the rising sun was taking charge of the day. The damp marine air was beginning to warm slightly, as I set out along the shoreline following the fluid path the waves made as they gently rolled onto the nearly deserted beach.

I recall another walker passing me in the opposite direction. His stride made an impression on me. Unlike mine, his was brisk and full of purpose, as he hauled some large pieces of trash toward a garbage can at the beach entrance. This man was clearly on a mission, where as I was on a journey.

The ocean had always been a spiritual retreat for me, and on this day, the surf and sand had a similar effect. As I walked with my head down, watching my feet strike the sand, I began to drift deep into thought, pondering the path my life had taken. I recalled specific times when I was faced with definite choices, and I began to mentally beat myself up over some of the decisions I had made. I asked myself, "Why had I chosen *that* road when it was clearly a bad decision? Why had I let others unduly influence my choices? Why was I experiencing rejection and defeat at every turn with my writing? Why was nothing measuring up to my expectation of it?"

Soon I was at the pinnacle of disenchantment and the depths of soul searching. Like everyone else on the planet, I had been through some difficult times, but up until this point in my ordinary life, I had never experienced emotional pain as much as this. A spiritual suffering seemed to sink to the very depths of my being. Clearly, my soul was crying out for help.

Suddenly there on the beach, at that very moment, Jesus Christ was with me. Instantly his loving, familiar presence permeated my thoughts and my being. It did not create a jarring reaction within me, but rather an instinctively calming one. Without effort, I completely surrendered into his loving embrace. His was a perfect love, and I reveled in the warmth of it. There was not a shadow of a doubt that it was indeed my Lord and Savior.

Although this experience was similar to the brief encounter I had when I was nineteen years old, when he revealed himself to warn and protect me when my friend was murdered, this time he remained with me for a much longer period. While the first time he alone spoke, this time there was an actual conversation between the two of us. During our walk together, our communication was effortless. It wasn't necessary to speak actual words because he anticipated and responded to my every thought and action, through what I can only describe as telepathy.

Immediately Jesus washed away my emotional pain and replaced it with peace. In rapid succession he showed me specific events from my life and told me that he been there every step of the way. He showed me that the signs were there, even if I had been unaware of them at the time. He explained that while I viewed many of my decisions as mistakes or missteps, they were actually all part of God's plan for my life. I was to quit beating myself up over the past. Instead, I was to focus on this very point in time. Jesus said that all roads in my life, bumpy, smooth, or otherwise, had led up to this very moment when he was ready to reveal a divine directive to me.

God wanted me to write a book about my spiritual journey and relay information he would reveal this very day, on this very beach. From now on, I was to do God's work and in doing so, my life would belong to God. Jesus made it clear that only by following through on God's directive and focusing on my creator would I find the gratification and success I was seeking from my endeavors. I had to put God first making him the center of my life. At that moment, there was nothing I desired to do more.

After searching down so many roads that held disappointments and false promises that left me feeling empty and unfulfilled, finally my life made sense and my direction was clear. Mere words cannot do justice in describing how it felt to be in God's presence. It was truly a mountaintop moment and with it came a sense of blessed relief and absolute confirmation.

Throughout my adult life, I had always felt from somewhere deep down inside that I hadn't found the path I was truly meant to walk. Suddenly, joyously, now I knew. I had a job to do for God, one that he had chosen me specifically for, one that only I could accomplish—me an ordinary person from the suburbs of Pittsburgh. But on that beach with Jesus Christ within me, walking and talking with me, I felt anything but ordinary. I felt uniquely special, unconditionally loved and truly liberated. It was a state of being I felt certain that everyone was meant to know and could achieve through a relationship with him.

Not only did Jesus pause to allow me to process and savor the revelations that were washing over me—he rejoiced with me! He wanted to relieve the pain I was suffering. He wanted to set my feet on a new path, the right path, and he wanted me to play a vital role in the process. His love and compassion for me seemed to know no bounds. Then Jesus led me still further down the beach and continued with the lessons that I was to later write about.

I knew that when preaching to his many followers during his ministry, Jesus often used simple situations from nature and everyday life to highlight a spiritual truth. The Gospels of the New Testament document many of these parables. During our walk on the beach, Jesus used a scattering of common shells to relate a lesson that he directed me to share with others. As we passed along the sandy shore, Jesus led me to a small tide pool and directed me to look at the variety of shells it contained. The tide was out, and the pool was drying up in the morning sun.

First Jesus showed me some shells that were completely smashed, their many fragmented pieces strewn haphazardly across the sand. Next, he showed me some shells that were clamped tightly shut, buried under the sand and standing water to varying depths. Then he showed me a larger number of shells that were in the process of opening, some only slightly, others wider and others wider still.

He directed me to one larger, pure white shell that was lying

entirely open on the sand apart from the others, closer to the water-
line, completely receptive to the gentle waves, which were rhythmi-
cally washing grains of sand in and out, in and out.

We paused to observe this one superb shell, as the sun brilliantly
illuminated its total openness and harmonious flow with the surrounding environment. Immediately I sensed a splendid surrender
and total trust in the shell's absolute openness to its creator. In that
moment, I longed to be that simple, solitary shell that spoke volumes
about how life is meant to be lived.

Then Jesus led me back to the other shells and explained the
parable in detail. He said that people on earth are like these shells.
The shattered shells are those who are utterly broken and defeated.
The buried shells are those who are completely closed off to the possibility that God exists or those who have chosen to reject him
entirely. The partially open shells are those who are in the process of
accepting the infinite possibilities of a life directed by God, the more
open the better. He motioned toward the pristine shell, which is
God's desire for all of us—to be absolutely open, completely receptive, and in the flow with God's will for our lives.

First we must identify the type of shell we are and take spiritual
action now, ever striving to be the remarkable, wide-open shell.

If we are the shattered shell, then we must admit defeat and turn
to him. For only God, our creator, can perfectly piece us back
together, smooth our ragged edges making us whole again, ready to
receive, embrace, and act on his will for our lives.

If we are the closed and buried shell, then somehow we must
summon the strength to wriggle from within, casting off our doubts
and disbelief and slowly rise out of the sand ready to receive God and
his abundant promise of a better way of life through doing his will.

If we reject God entirely and are satisfied to remain the completely closed shell buried in the sand or lying on an earthly beach
soaking up the sun, then our eternal outlook is bleak. It is a straight-
forward message delivered with love and compassion. There are no
free rides into heaven. Our sin is what separates us from God, and we
must be willing to repent and start anew through forgiveness, *"for all
have sinned and fall short of the glory of God."* Romans 3:23

God sent his only son, Jesus Christ, to die on an earthly cross
and pay the ultimate penalty for those sins, so that separation from
God would no longer exist. In the Gospel of John 14:6–7 Jesus said,

"I am the way and the truth and the life. No one comes to the Father except through me. If you really knew me, you would know my Father as well. From now on you do know him and have seen him." We each have a choice to make.

If we are the partially open shell, then regardless of the degree to which we are already open to God, we must push out from within with all the might we can muster and open ourselves still further, until we are the wide-open shell, freely flowing with his will for our lives. This includes the closet Christians, like I was, those who are satisfied to remain sealed inside our secure little shells with our faith, only opening up the slightest bit to share our beliefs in the safest of settings. If it takes a crowbar, then we must find one and boldly pry ourselves open, bravely putting the courage of our convictions out into the world because we have seen the light and know the truth. We must gratefully receive God's gift, get past any reservations we have, and faithfully share it with others.

As Christians, it is not good enough to secure our own eternal salvation and then close up safely inside our shells, neglecting our duty to share the Good News of Jesus Christ with non-believers. Salvation is available to everyone—anytime, anywhere. There is but one simple choice to make on earth and an eternity in heaven to reap the rewards.

God longs to transform everyone, right here, right now, but many are deaf, dumb and blind to his truth. In the Gospel of Matthew 13:13–17 Jesus said, *"This is why I speak to them in parables: Though seeing, they do not see; though hearing, they do not hear or understand. In them is fulfilled the prophecy of Isaiah: You will be ever hearing but never understanding; you will be ever seeing but never perceiving. For this people's heart has become callused; they hardly hear with their ears, and they have closed their eyes. Otherwise they might see with their eyes, hear with their ears, understand with their hearts and turn, and I would heal them."*

We mustn't let a calcified heart keep us from an intimate relationship with a very real, living Lord. The process of opening our shell begins with a sincere desire from the heart to truly know him. Each person must invite God into their life by accepting Jesus Christ as their Lord and Savior.

In the Gospel of Matthew 7:7–8 Jesus said, *"Ask and it will be given to you; seek and you will find; knock and the door will be opened to you. For everyone who asks receives; he who seeks finds; and to him who knocks, the door will be opened."* I believe that God wants us to do a lot more asking, seeking and knocking. Not doing so is like having the keys to a glorious mansion and choosing to remain living in a tattered, cardboard box. Even for a child, the novelty of a fresh refrigerator box wears off after a few adventures in make-believe.

Unfortunately, many people think that God is make-believe. I am here to tell those people that the times when Jesus Christ supernaturally revealed himself in my life were more real than any experience I have ever known, before or since.

Whatever we must individually do to become the completely open shell in the flow with our creator, one thing is certain, our individual process won't be easy or pain free. It requires our total trust and absolute surrender to God's will.

I believe that faith is what keeps our opening shell on top of the sand and allows us to weather the storms of life that rage around us threatening to bury us in the sand. Once we stride that first step toward faith and accept Jesus Christ's open invitation into our lives, we will never be the same and there will be no turning back. Once we turn our life over to God, he will faithfully lead us day by day to do his will, if we sincerely strive to be the wide-open, superb shell. When we do our part, as difficult as it may be, God will surely do his. The rewards will be more immense than we can imagine and the truly good life for us will begin. *"For it is by grace you have been saved, through faith—and this is not from yourselves, it is the gift of God—not by works, so that no one can boast. For we are God's workmanship, created in Christ Jesus to do good works, which God prepared in advance for us to do."* Ephesians 2:8–10

The process of completely opening our shell is a dynamic one and a life long journey. Throughout that journey, there will surely be times when we are more open to God's will than at other times. Regardless of the state of our shell, our divine directive remains the same—to become the pristine shell completely open to God's will for our lives. How wonderful it is to have such a patient and loving Heavenly Father, who is willing to remain steadfastly beside us every step of the way! Though we may waver, God does not.

While we may never fully become that pristine shell during our lifetime, the more we allow ourselves to open up to God's will, the more joyful and fulfilling our earthly lives will become. God wants each of us to start living the truly good life he has in store for us today.

In the Book of Romans 12: 2 the Apostle Paul wrote, *"Don't copy the behavior and customs of this world, but let God transform you into a new person by changing the way you think. Then you will know what God wants you to do, and you will know how good and pleasing and perfect his will really is."* The Lord's transforming love is available to all who seek it

As our walk continued, the parable of the shells began to sink in. When I grew fearful that I might forget important details, Jesus lovingly reassured me and told me not to worry.

I had become so completely engrossed in the interaction with him that I didn't see what lay ahead. Up until that point, the entire experience was remarkable and perfect in every way, in all that he revealed about my life, in the lessons that he taught, in the divine directive that he gave and in the unconditional love and support that he offered freely and unconditionally. Now I was in for another awesome surprise.

As we continued along the shoreline, the beach curved slightly to the right. We paused for a moment, and I gathered my thoughts. When I finally looked up, there in front of us, illuminated by the sun was the glorious snowcapped Olympic Mountain Range stretched out in its full magnificent splendor. I was absolutely awestruck. My breath caught in my chest, as I soaked in the dazzling beauty and power displayed before us. The first thought that leapt to mind was that I hadn't even known it was possible to see the mountains from here, and yet here they were. This was a place I had never been before, both literally and figuratively. How could I have missed them? Suddenly I felt foolish.

As these thoughts swirled in my mind, Jesus said, "Remember Susan, you don't always have to see the mountains to know that they are there." I repeated his words aloud, branding them on my brain. As his words began to sink in, I realized that his presence was gone.

I gazed at the mammoth mountains awhile longer, pondering the meaning of those parting words. Then I turned back toward the way I had come. The walk back would be far different than the walk there. With each step I took, I repeated Christ's parting words repeatedly. Each time I said them, my steps grew lighter, and my heart grew fuller. This time, I held my head high, rejoicing. I was no longer in despair, wallowing in self-doubt and tormented by emotional pain.

Jesus himself had delivered me from the depths of soul searching, had relieved my suffering, opened my eyes, rejuvenated my spirit and set my feet on solid ground. He had shown me the way to joy and fulfillment. What a difference a half an hour makes when that time is spent with the Lord! Now my life had real purpose.

By the time I reached the beach entrance, I thought my heart would burst from happiness. It had been so long since I felt anything even remotely close to joy that I found the experience to be almost overwhelming. Stepping from the sand of the beach onto the concrete of the street, I inhaled deeply, held my breath and turned to take a last look at the setting where my life's purpose truly began. I exhaled with conviction, knowing that I would hold this experience in my heart, mind and soul until the day I leave this earth.

Jesus didn't explain his parting words to me in detail, as he had the parable of the shells. I wish I could say that the full meaning was immediately clear. Months later, when doubts began to creep back into my life, I continued to reflect on his words and realized a much deeper and lasting meaning. I felt foolish all over again, that I had been so entangled in my own problems that I failed to see it that glorious day on the beach with God.

The walk with Jesus was a mountaintop moment for me. It was the pinnacle of my spiritual journey in my otherwise ordinary life. Yet, as moving and as life changing as that experience was and as much as I wanted to remain on the crystal clear mountaintop with God, I couldn't. Eventually I found myself down off the mountaintop in the real world below.

I realized that these types of spiritual experiences would be the exception rather than the rule. There would again be times in my life when I would venture off course, feel lost and unable to sense God's presence. Christ's parting words reminded me that we don't always have to experience God to know that he is there. It's about having faith, and a little faith goes a long way. In the Gospel of Luke 17:5–6, *"The apostles said to the Lord, "Increase our faith!" He replied, "If you have faith as small as a mustard seed, you can say to this mulberry tree, 'Be uprooted and planted in the sea,' and it will obey you."* With God, all things are possible.

God has an amazing and surprising spiritual journey in store for each and every one of us, if we will only put our faith in him. Faith is our lifeline to our loving God, but first we must make the choice to grab a hold and hang on with all of our might. Thanks be to God.

I will praise you, O Lord, with all my heart;
I will tell of all your wonders.
I will be glad and rejoice in you;
I will sing praise to your name,
O Most High.

Psalm 9:1–2

AN INVITATION

For God so loved the world that he gave his one and only Son,
that whoever believes in him shall not perish but have eternal life.

John 3:16

That if you confess with your mouth, "Jesus is Lord,"
and believe in your heart that God raised him from the dead,
you will be saved."

Romans 10:9

The way to know God is through Jesus Christ. God sent his Son into the world so that we would know how deeply God desires a relationship with us. He did not stand away from us; God drew near to us and gave us his most beloved Son so that we would know God's love.

Jesus also willingly gave his life on the cross, but did not stay in the grave. Three days later, he was resurrected and then revealed himself to over five hundred people. Forty days later, he returned to heaven, where he waits to take God's people to heaven for eternity.

This is good news. A relationship with Jesus is available to you. Your response is one of faith, nothing else! If you desire to know Jesus and follow him, you can pray this sample prayer. When you pray it, you become Jesus' follower for eternity. Nothing you can do will ever make him stop loving you. This is grace.

"God, thank you for sending your Son, Jesus Christ, to
earth so that I could know how deeply you love me. I

*believe that Jesus is your Son and that he died for my
sins, and then he was resurrected from the dead, so he
lives today. I want to follow him. Thank you for the
invitation to be part of your family. I want to know you
better.*

Amen."

If you made the decision to invite Jesus to be part of your life, congratulations! This is the most important decision you will ever make in your life. Don't try to live your life of faith in Jesus alone: find a church where you can meet other Christ followers and learn what God says in his word, the Bible.

If you email me, I will pray for you, as you begin the great adventure of faith in Jesus Christ.

Pastor Tamara Buchan

tamarab@plcc.org

Deeper in Christ...
Further in Mission

The Evangelical Covenant Church (ECC) is a rapidly growing multi-ethnic denomination in the United States and Canada with ministries on five continents of the world. Founded in 1885 by Swedish Immigrants, the ECC values the Bible as the Word of God, the gift of God's grace and ever-deepening spiritual life that comes through faith in Jesus Christ, the importance of extending God's love and compassion to a hurting world, and the strength that comes from unity within diversity.

To find out more about The Evangelical Covenant Church denomination or to find a church near you, visit www.covchurch.org or contact The Evangelical Covenant Church, 5101 N. Francisco Ave., Chicago, IL 60625, (773) 784-3000.